What people are s:
The Sensational

"Don't let the title of the book fool you—the lessons within these pages will help you with every aspect of your life. I couldn't put it down—I kept wanting to know the next lesson to be learned. Informative and entertaining. I'm ready for the next book in the series."
—Greg Laird, Esq., founding partner,
United in Motion Global Sports
Management Company

"*The Sensational Salesman* presents a revolutionary approach to sales that will restore the reputation of salespersons everywhere. Duane Cummings delivers golden nuggets of sales wisdom that will transform your results forever. A must-read for anyone in sales."
—Trish Carr, author of *It's Just a Conversation:
What to Say and How to Say It in Business.*

"Compelling, thought-provoking, and instructive, this modern-day business parable is a page-turner. It is rich with powerful ideas about what it takes to succeed in sales and in life. Its message will stay with you long after you finish reading this powerful book."
—Ava Diamond, leadership and employee engagement
speaker and CEO, Ava Diamond International

"I wholeheartedly believe *The Sensational Salesman* should be mandatory reading for every entrepreneur, or anyone looking to improve their life for that matter! I use many of the lessons everyday. The information is easy to understand and if you apply what you learn, you can see the positive results immediately."
-Taylor Hanna, Fashion Designer and Trend
Setter, CEO, The Clad Stache

The —— SENSATIONAL SALESMAN

A Second Chance Story:
Providing a Simple Path to Improving
Your Relationships, Career, and Life

DUANE CUMMINGS

BALBOA
PRESS

A DIVISION OF HAY HOUSE

Balboa Press books may be ordered through booksellers or by contacting:

Balboa Press
A Division of Hay House
1663 Liberty Drive
Bloomington, IN 47403
www.balboapress.com
1 (877) 407-4847

Because of the dynamic nature of the Internet, any web addresses or links contained in this book may have changed since publication and may no longer be valid. The views expressed in this work are solely those of the author and do not necessarily reflect the views of the publisher, and the publisher hereby disclaims any responsibility for them.

The author of this book does not dispense medical advice or prescribe the use of any technique as a form of treatment for physical, emotional, or medical problems without the advice of a physician, either directly or indirectly. The intent of the author is only to offer information of a general nature to help you in your quest for emotional and spiritual well-being. In the event you use any of the information in this book for yourself, which is your constitutional right, the author and the publisher assume no responsibility for your actions.

Any people depicted in stock imagery provided by Thinkstock are models, and such images are being used for illustrative purposes only.
Certain stock imagery © Thinkstock.

Print information available on the last page.

ISBN: 978-1-5043-2842-5 (sc)
ISBN: 978-1-5043-2844-9 (hc)
ISBN: 978-1-5043-2843-2 (e)

Library of Congress Control Number: 2015903044

Balboa Press rev. date: 02/26/2015

This book is dedicated to my loving wife Kim, and my two amazing sons Matthew and Christopher.

CONTENTS

CHAPTER 1

All this was new to me. Life takes us by surprise and orders us to move towards the unknown—even when we don't want to and we think we don't need to.

—Paulo Coelho

A Day Like No Other

It was just before 9:00 a.m. on Thursday and Thomas Frickle was in the parking lot of Discount Golf, waiting for the doors to open. He was there to pick up a dozen golf balls and take a few swings in their new state-of-the-art simulator. After that he was meeting three guys for a round at his favorite course. The trip was thirty miles out of the way, but since the company he worked for, Harvey, McGill & Harper, provided him a car and gas to use, he didn't think twice about making the journey. In fact, if anyone at work asked where he was this morning, he had the perfect answer. Right down the street from the golf shop were the offices of National Contractors Inc., a potential customer his company had been targeting. Every previous salesperson had tried getting in the door, but no one had succeeded. Thomas thought, *If someone asks why I wasn't available this morning, I'll say I went by their offices again. It'll show I'm being persistent and trying to get the account open.* He smiled at his own ingenuity.

1

Thomas had organized the golf outing to help celebrate what was going to be the biggest week of his life. The following night he was proposing to his girlfriend, Sandy Hill. He and Sandy had dated for three years. She was twenty-six and had taught fifth grade since receiving her degree in education two years earlier. Thomas was twenty-seven and put himself through college after his parents kicked him out of the house. Initially he struggled on his own, but he finally finished a business degree and then bounced around between a dozen sales jobs before landing in his current position. The following Tuesday would mark his one-year anniversary with the company. Sandy and Thomas's relationship had been pretty rocky in the beginning, mainly due to his irresponsible decisions and actions. Then things leveled out and seemed to be headed in the right direction with the stability of this job and the recent purchase of a new house.

Unfortunately, some of his recent decisions—today's golf outing, recently skipping work to tend to his new house, canceling two appointments the previous day to purchase the engagement ring—were not of the quality that had helped him create the life he was living and proud of. He and Sandy had been shopping many times and he knew which ring she had her heart set on. To pay for the ring, Thomas spent the remainder of his savings and most of the money in his checking account—and he used the only credit card he had left that wasn't already maxed out. He had also spent a ton of money to furnish the house. Now, with a nice place to live and a beautiful ring, Thomas felt as though he had set the stage for a long, happy marriage.

Thomas arrived at the golf course to find his buddies unloading their bags. They went to the clubhouse to check in and Thomas happily announced he would pick up the tab for everyone. He paid with the company credit card, figuring he'd turn it in on his expense account. Thomas thought if he told people he took the managers of the Bohemian Construction Company out to play golf, they'd believe him. Bohemian was a large, longtime customer of Harvey,

McGill & Harper, and though he was assigned to the account and getting credit for their sales, they usually preferred to deal with Mr. Harvey directly. With his receipt in hand, he headed out of the pro shop with the happy group.

As the four stood waiting at the first tee, Thomas did what any respectable golfer would: he turned his cell phone off and placed it in his golf bag. Then he pulled out the ring to show everyone. The guys were stunned at the size of the stone and all agreed he had made a good choice. He tucked it in his bag and stepped up to hit away.

After the round, the friends all went their separate ways. Before leaving the course, Thomas checked his voice mail. There was only one message, from Mr. Harvey. "I have some good news and I want to share it with you. Not to worry, we can discuss it tomorrow after our meeting. Have a nice evening." There was always a Friday morning meeting that usually lasted about three hours; every department was represented. The sales updates were typically done at the end, but perhaps Thomas would get to hear Mr. Harvey's news before then.

The next day, Thomas sat in the meeting daydreaming about his pending engagement until it was his turn to report. He briefly went over his top accounts and gave the usual update, filled with fluff. To cover his tracks for the week, since he had been dealing with a lot of personal business on company time, he fibbed and said he had stopped in at the offices of National Contractors and tried to make headway with the President, Mr. Donald. Thomas said, "Mr. Donald blew me off as usual, but I'll keep trying." He also added, "And yesterday, I took the managers from Bohemian out to play golf. They are getting ready to place a large order and I'm told we're on the short list to supply it."

The room looked surprised. Mr. McGill raised his eyebrows with interest. Thomas had been hoping for something to go his way, since his sales had been flat for the first six months after arriving at the company, and the last five months they had taken a bit of a downturn. He would regularly justify the situation by reminding himself that it wasn't as though the other salesmen were setting any records either—it's a tough market out there. Marcus Wiley had been sitting next to Thomas during the meeting and was now smiling from ear to ear. It was out of character, since Fridays normally brought a frown to his face. He hated long meetings and preferred being out in the field. Marcus had always been jealous of Thomas for being given the Bohemian account. In fact, the entire office viewed the assignment of that account as a form of charity, and everyone believed it was income that Thomas didn't really earn.

Immediately after Thomas finished his report, Mr. Harvey nodded to his partners and spoke up. "Please excuse us for a few minutes, I'd like to take a quick break. We'll be back to conclude the meeting in fifteen minutes" Mr. Harvey, Mr. McGill, and Mr. Harper headed down the hall to Mr. Harvey's office. The rest of the group retreated to the break room to devour doughnuts that had been dropped off by a vendor.

A few minutes later, the receptionist, Ms. Lee, entered and pointed to Thomas. "Your presence is requested in Mr. Harvey's office."

While heading down the hall Thomas smiled to himself and thought, *I've been here a year and it looks like I'm finally going to get that raise. This must be what the phone message Mr. Harvey left me was about.*

As he entered the office, Thomas noticed Mr. Jones, the Human Resources manager, sitting in the corner. He thought, *It makes sense. He's here to go over my pay raise.*

Mr. McGill said, "Go ahead and sit down, Thomas. So, you made some progress yesterday?"

Thomas replied, "I think so. I believe it's only a matter of time before National Contractors gets on board with us, and I'm hoping to land that Bohemian Construction order."

The other gentlemen looked at each other. Mr. Harvey stepped forward. "Thomas, I think deep down you are a good young man, but unfortunately it seems you've decided to make some poor choices."

Thomas was visibly shaken. A look of bewilderment crossed his face. *This doesn't sound like the start of a conversation about my one-year pay raise*, he thought.

Mr. McGill stood and moved toward Thomas. "We find it fairly hard to believe you spoke to Mr. Donald yesterday, or played golf with any of the managers from Bohemian."

Thomas tried to collect himself. "And why is that?" he asked innocently.

"Because they were all here in our offices finalizing the details of a joint venture. Just after lunch we got a call from Mr. Donald about a project they wanted to perform, but they needed the expertise of the Bohemian guys. Mr. Harvey put together an emergency meeting here at our offices with everyone whom you claimed to have seen or spent time with recently in attendance. When asked, they all admitted they hadn't seen you in weeks."

Mr. Harvey chimed in, "I called your cell phone to try to get you involved before they all arrived here, but I couldn't reach you." The silence that followed was deafening.

Mr. Jones stood and spoke. "It's unfortunate, but this will be your last day with us. You know very well it is against our company policy to lie, and that's exactly what you did. Come with me, and I will help you gather your things. We'll need your company phone, your laptop, and the keys to your vehicle. We have arranged for a taxi to take you home. I think you will find we're being more than generous by giving you two weeks' severance along with any unpaid vacation or sick days you have accrued." He motioned for Thomas to rise and follow him. As Thomas stepped to the door, he looked back to find the three gentlemen shaking their heads in disappointment.

Thomas's trip home in the taxi was a blur. Full of shame, he never once looked the driver in the eyes. He pushed his front door open, dropped his stuff, and went straight to the bathroom to throw up.

He lay on the tile floor, paralyzed with fear. Thoughts whirled through his head. *What will happen to my house? What will I use for transportation? How will I pay for the furniture? What about my credit cards? And that ring, how in the world can I quickly find another job where I could make enough money to finish paying for that huge ring? I just got fired and everyone's going to know it.*

Thomas had recently called Sandy's father asking permission to marry her, and that conversation kept ringing in his head. Then he made reservations for tonight at the most exclusive restaurant in the city. With the engagement looming, he stood up, stared in the mirror, and addressed himself. "You brought this on yourself. You got so far off track from the way you were raised. You're reaping what you sowed."

He washed his face in the basin, thinking, *Pull yourself together and make sure things go perfectly tonight. Do what you have to do and don't ruin this evening. You can fix everything later. You've been through tough times before and came out okay. You can do this.* With a new look of confidence, he went to take a shower and prepare for what he had anticipated being the most important night of his life.

Thomas had a couple of hours before he was supposed to meet Sandy. She was going straight from school to get her nails done with a friend who was in on the plan. The accomplice was going to get Sandy to the restaurant and then disappear. They had planned a "special girls' adventure." Of course, when you propose, you do all you can to keep it a surprise. But Thomas was pretty sure Sandy knew something was up. Too many things had given away the fact that tonight might be a setup. He thought she had overheard him on the phone confirming the dinner reservations, and he also suspected that Sandy's mother had accidentally let the cat out of the bag.

Luckily, since the company took his cell phone, Thomas still had a home phone. He called Mark, one of the guys he had played golf with the day before, and asked him for a ride. He would probably have to call a cab to get Sandy home that night, but he could use "having a drink" as an excuse. *If someone gets nosy,* Thomas thought,

I'll just say the company car is in the shop and break the news about getting fired at a better time.

Mark picked him up and dropped him off at the restaurant just in time to bump into Sandy at the door. Her friend was supposedly going to park the car, but true to the plan, she drove out of sight.

Sandy laughed when she saw Thomas. "I had a feeling something was up." They entered the restaurant and the maître d' quickly seated them. Thomas ordered a bottle of wine.

As he and Sandy sipped their wine, he heard a familiar voice. "Good to see you Mario," he heard Mr. Harvey say. He was seated at a table with Marcus Wiley and gentlemen from both Bohemian Construction and National Contractors. Marcus noticed the couple and gave Thomas a thumbs-up as he put his arm around Mr. Donald. Thomas tried to contain his embarrassment and anger as he focused his attention on his beautiful bride-to-be.

Marcus was noticeably giddy and kept winking and nodding. After a few minutes, he rose and approached the couple, relishing the opportunity to embarrass Thomas in front of his girl. It was in his nature to kick someone while they were down, and he saw a huge opportunity. Marcus introduced himself to Sandy, then quickly turned to Thomas and said loudly, "It's a pity you were let go today, sport. Probably should be a little more truthful at your next place of employment." He turned his attention to Sandy, who looked astonished. "Oh, I'm sorry, I thought you would have heard already." Then he walked confidently backed to his table with a devilish grin.

Thomas wanted to get up and slug Marcus, but that would only have made matters worse. Besides, Sandy had begun to cry. She stared at Thomas.

"I can explain—"

Sandy put her hand up and snapped, "Just stop! Honesty, that's all I asked of you. We promised each other no secrets and no lies."

"What do you want me to say? I was trying not to hurt you."

She blurted, "So you lied?"

His heart sank. "Yes, I lost my job and had to get a ride here—they took the company car." He leaned forward, pleading with her. "I'll figure out something, I always do."

Sandy's lips were quivering and she was trying to hold herself together. She shook her head. "I truly thought you had changed."

Thomas knew there would be no engagement now. Sandy didn't say another word. She rose from the table and walked out of the restaurant, never looking back. He wanted to chase after her, but he thought it would make things worse.

Shattered, he finally stood, left some money on the table, and slipped out of the room quietly. He lingered in the doorway for a minute, trying to determine his next move. He lived thirty minutes away, had no car, no cell phone, and it was pouring rain. He pushed the door open, defeated, and walked out into the rain. He thought about taking a cab, but he figured he needed to save every dime. In a feeble attempt to stay dry, he pulled his jacket over his head and started down the deserted sidewalk.

After walking about a block, Thomas was startled when someone honked behind him. He looked back just in time to be doused by a passing vehicle plowing through a puddle. Thomas cleared the water from his face and saw a shiny black Range Rover pull to the curb and screech to a halt ahead of him. The brake lights illuminated the tag, which read SNSATNL. A man got out of the SUV, popped open an umbrella, and ran toward Thomas. He was of medium height and had short hair.

The man said, "I am truly sorry. I tried to swerve, but almost hit another car." The man used the umbrella to shelter Thomas from the rain, but he was already soaked. "Look, I really am sorry."

Thomas tried to shake off some of the water. "It's okay. As weird as it may sound, I probably had it coming."

The man gave Thomas a puzzled look. "Can I drop you somewhere—anywhere?" He opened the door and motioned for Thomas to get into the vehicle. "It's the least I can do." He motioned again and looked to the sky. "C'mon, get in. I won't take no for an answer."

Thomas took a long look at the man, and then stepped into the SUV and the man shut the door. He quickly went around the vehicle, closed his umbrella, and climbed in behind the wheel. "So, where to?"

"Just up a couple of blocks, please. I think there's a bus stop there."

The man shook his head. "No bus tonight. Not after the super soaking I gave you. Let me drop you off at home, if that's where you're headed."

Thomas wiped his face with his sleeve. "Thanks for the offer, but I can take the bus. I live a long way away."

"Why don't you let me decide if it's a long way," the man retorted.

Thomas sighed. "I live out in Cheshire Heights—you know where that is?"

The man beamed. "You bet, I have to go right by there. My house is on the lake. So, it's no trouble at all and you'll be home and dry before you know it." He reached for his cell phone and dialed a number. "Hello, beautiful. Yeah, it's coming down hard here too. Just wanted to let you know I'm going to be a bit late. No, no problems." He smiled at Thomas. "Just helping someone out. I'll call you when I get close. Love you too." He shut the phone off.

Thomas stammered, "I really appreciate this. Most people wouldn't have stopped, let alone offered a ride."

The man turned to Thomas, and with the look of someone who has been in a bind before, said, "Well, my good man, you're probably right. But I'm not most people." As he flipped on his turn signal, checked his mirrors and headed out into traffic, he added, "And I believe everything happens for a reason, so there's probably more to this than currently meets the eye."

He reached to adjust the heating controls and asked, "Warm enough?"

Thomas ran his hands in front of the vents. "Yes, it feels good. Thanks again."

The man smiled and then said with a quizzical look, "Can I ask you something?"

"Sure." Thomas pulled his jacket tight.

"I mean, you don't have to answer, but I'd love to know your story." Thomas began to fidget and squirm and the man saw how uneasy he was with the question. "I didn't mean to make you uncomfortable. I just thought that a guy like you, walking downtown in the rain at night, looking to take the bus to Cheshire Heights—well, you must have some kind of a story, and I thought it would be an interesting way to pass the time." Thomas looked like a turtle as his head shrunk down into his jacket.

A red light forced the man to pull to a stop as a bolt of lightning cracked across the sky. He turned to Thomas. "Look, I realize we just met, and if I'm prying, I apologize. You'd be well within your rights not to tell me anything." He waited for the light to change and slowly accelerated.

Thomas said, "I don't mean to be disrespectful. You just caught me at the end of the worst day of my life and I'd prefer not to relive it."

"Wow, I am sorry to hear that. So, I guess my drenching you was just the icing on the cake?" Thomas nodded. "Well, as weird as this may sound, I have a strong feeling that something awesome could come out of all this! All my greatest triumphs came after disasters."

Thomas replied, "The truth is, I probably don't deserve having something great happen to me. I realized tonight that I've become the kind of person I despise. I'm not sure when or how it happened, but it did. I'm pretty sure I was a good guy at one time in my life." He took a deep breath and stared blankly out the windshield.

The man broke the silence. "How about this—since I'm the one who enjoys talking, would it be okay if I told you my story?" He seemed eager. "I'll start, and if I begin to put you to sleep, you can stop me. Would that work?" Thomas relaxed a bit and nodded his assent.

"Well, okay, then. I guess I'll start at the beginning. But let me warn you, just about every person I've told my story to ends up becoming a part of my life in some way. So, last chance. You can still back out."

"The least I can do is listen, since you are giving me a ride," Thomas assured him. "I'm sure your story is better than anything I would have to say right now."

The man flashed a broad smile. "Well, who knows, maybe we can change that? Let's get this journey started!"

CHAPTER 2

No legacy is so rich as Honesty.

—William Shakespeare

A Foundation Built on Honesty and Integrity

The man began, "My name is Bradford Williams. But growing up, I was known to most people as B.W., B. Willy, or the infamous Mr. Troublemaker. I'm forty-one and I'm an Aquarius." He turned with a smile to Thomas, who let a small grin slip across his face. Bradford added, "Just making sure you're listening." He quickly gained a serious, concerned look and gave Thomas a consoling pat on the shoulder.

Then he began again, this time with a firm, fatherly voice. "My friends call me Brad. I've lived in the city all my life. I was orphaned at the age of four when my mother died of a drug overdose. She was a prostitute and she never knew who my father was." Thomas sat up a little straighter and began to give the storyteller the respect he was due. Brad signaled, entered the expressway, and began to leave the city behind.

The rain continued, and without the city lights, Brad's face was hardly visible, but his voice rang true and clear. "I was moved from foster home to foster home. I went to a juvenile detention center more times than I can count. Let's see, I stole, drank, took drugs, got into fights, and finally dropped out of school in the ninth grade—"

"You're just messing with me again, right?" Thomas interrupted. He was now firmly engaged.

Brad shook his head. "No, all of it's true, and luckily, that's who I *was*! Yes, I said *was*. Although I'm not proud of my past, it is *my* past. No matter how embarrassing it is to tell people, I have to own it and be totally honest. The day I learned that lesson is when my life changed forever." Thomas turned in his seat, now eager to hear more.

Brad continued, "It's ironic, though, I begin telling you the truth about my life and you think I'm messing with you or lying. I guess it's true that fiction is sometimes easier to believe than fact. There was a time when I couldn't tell the difference between my lies and the truth. Thankfully, that all changed the day of my twenty-eighth birthday." Brad dropped his head and hunched his shoulders in a sign of regret. "It was a hell of a day." Brad took a long, deep breath. "Maybe just like yours was today?" Thomas was now fully engaged and enthralled by what Brad had to say.

Brad raised his head proudly and continued, "Since that day, I've changed my life around. I'm sober, I'm drug free, I went back and finished high school, and yes, I went to college. I am happily married, I have three wonderful children, tons of fantastic friends, and I'm the owner of or a partner in several successful companies." Brad nodded and raised his eyebrows. "Bet you didn't expect to hear that story from me?" Thomas turned his head slowly from side to side in disbelief. Brad turned on his signal as they passed a sign that read CHESHIRE HEIGHTS, NEXT EXIT.

They came to a stop at the bottom of the off-ramp. Brad leaned into Thomas while waiting for the light to change, "Want to know what I owe my turnaround to? What took me from wasting my life away to having it all?"

Thomas nodded. "Yes, I would."

Brad whispered for effect. "Honesty and Integrity!" He sat back as Thomas contemplated the enormousness of the simple explanation. "Yeah, I know, it sounds ridiculous and almost preachy, but those two things were the foundation that I built my new life on. Those two traits are what have allowed me to have a Sensational Life now."

Thomas's eyes began to dart around as if searching his mind for information. You could tell what Brad said had struck a chord in him. It was as if something was working its way to the surface. They came to the main entrance of Cheshire Heights and Brad turned to Thomas. "There aren't many stories as bad as mine. Not many more embarrassing. But, by being honest and telling it, I can give hope to others."

"Well, after the day I had, hope is something I could definitely use."

Brad interrupted. "So, what's your address?"

Thomas guided the duo through the neighborhood and they came to a stop in front of his house. Brad turned off the vehicle. The rain had stopped and the stillness and quiet were calming.

Brad spoke, "So, safe and sound at home. But I am going to take a shot and guess you are really not much better off than when I picked you up in the city." Thomas nodded in agreement. Brad continued, "I have a weird feeling that the events that happened tonight could be a huge turning point in your life story." He looked deep into Thomas's eyes. "So, is there any chance you'll ever share your story with me?"

Brad asked in such a way that Thomas felt a wave of pure love and concern emitting from this stranger. "I appreciate what you've done for me tonight," he said. "You've been so kind. Honestly, I don't deserve to be treated this well."

Brad sat forward and exclaimed, "Well, now, there is a start. One out of two, there is hope." It took a second for this to sink into Thomas's still wet head, and then he laughed. "I did say *honestly*, didn't I? So, perhaps you are right and maybe it would help to talk it out."

14

Brad replied, "I think we would both agree that this chance meeting is only half over. But, I'm sorry to say, I can't continue it tonight. My family is waiting for me. So, why don't we agree on a time to pick it back up?"

Thomas nodded in easy agreement. "You know, I don't think it could hurt."

Brad started his car. "Do you have plans for tomorrow?"

Thomas didn't have to think long. "No, I guess I don't."

"Well, how about eight in the morning? I already know where you live—I'll pick you up right here." Brad offered his hand. "So, until tomorrow."

Thomas shook hands, shut the door, and watched as Brad quickly disappeared. *That was definitely a hell of a day,* he thought.

Thomas tossed and turned all night and was lying in his bed, wide awake, when the alarm went off at seven. As he reached to shut off the alarm, he noticed the ring box on his nightstand and remembered every horrible detail of the previous day. Slowly he sat up, wondering why he had agreed to meet so early on a Saturday and take a surprise trip with a total stranger. *I'm not sure why this guy wants to get to know me better, but I might as well see this through and find out where it ends,* he thought. He threw the covers back, still dressed in his clothes from the night before. He slowly wiped the sleep from his eyes and stretched.

Thomas had no idea what this day was going to bring, but he wanted to be ready when Brad arrived. He got out of bed, showered, dressed, and decided to sit out on his front porch to wait. As he went through the events from the previous day, he couldn't believe how his life had changed in a matter of hours. He thought about going back into the house and calling Sandy. After a few minutes of pondering, he figured it was too soon—he really needed to be clear on what he would say when he did call. Just as promised, Brad pulled up on time and waved for Thomas to get in.

Thomas couldn't hold back a hard yawn as he got in the vehicle. "Excuse me—sorry about that."

Brad snickered, backed out of the driveway, and sped off. "So, didn't get a good nights sleep?"

Thomas rubbed his bloodshot eyes. "Not really."

Brad's face turned serious. "Well, I slept like a baby and I have for thirteen years. Yesterday is gone and today is a new day. The only thing you can do about the past is to learn from it. So, my first question for you is, What did you learn from what happened yesterday?"

Thomas scratched his head and began to reply, "Actually, I hadn't thought about it that way, but now that you mention it—"

"What is it?" Brad asked curtly.

"That you were probably right on the money when you said that honesty is the foundation for living a sensational life. I was mistaken and thought I had a great life. But it all fell apart in the blink of an eye, because I stopped being truthful and honest, especially with myself.

"You know, if I had been honest, I would probably still have a job and would be engaged right now. The sad thing is that I didn't need to lie about any of it."

Brad nodded. "You know that everyone has both good and bad habits, right? And, unfortunately, lying is a bad habit a lot of people have. People talk about breaking bad habits all the time. In reality, people just swap one habit for another. Think about it: if someone stops drinking, maybe they take up smoking. If they stop smoking, they start overeating. They are searching for a habit that gives them pleasure and helps them avoid pain. Well, I found that telling the truth could bring me the most happiness, and so I made the decision never to lie again, not even little white lies. I have never looked back."

Brad looked at Thomas sharply. "So, now you're saying you truly understand that honesty is the foundation? But do you think you can commit to a total change?"

Thomas replied with confidence, "I know I can."

"Talk is cheap," Brad retorted. "You have to be fed up with the pain you caused yourself and others. If you are, decide now and be done with it." He pounded the dash. "Just *commit* and get on with your new life!"

The pounding startled Thomas, but he sat up confidently and said, "You're right! Okay, let's do it." He tapped his head with his finger. "I know now that no matter how hard a person wants to forget their past and all the mistakes they made, they'll never escape it. So, rather than lie and try to pretend it didn't happen, I'm going to follow your example and embrace it. I'll find a way to use it for good."

"That's right, keep going."

"The way you spoke when we first met made it seem like honesty was easier than lying. It's weird, you had a horrible past, but you weren't embarrassed to tell me and it didn't keep you from becoming successful. You have inspired me to start telling nothing but the truth. I think it's time I tell my story from the beginning!"

"Remember though, you can't change your past, but your future is totally up to you," Brad said. "You create your future by the decisions you make today."

"Then my future will be great, I promise," Thomas declared.

"I appreciate you saying that to me, but the worst lying a person can do is to themselves," Brad replied. "The only person you need to make that promise to is you, and then follow through by keeping that promise." He pulled the car into a neighborhood park that was badly overgrown and dirty. The playground equipment was dilapidated and trash was strewn everywhere. There were several other cars in the parking lot and about a dozen people in matching green T-shirts were standing in a circle. "Well, I guess the secret's out," he observed. "A little community service work—you don't mind, do you?" Thomas shook his head and smiled brightly.

Several of the people in the group turned and motioned to Brad. He gave an energetic wave and greeted them. "Morning, all." An older man approached them with an armload of trash bags, shovels, and rakes. Brad took some of the items from him. "Good morning, Mr. Hyatt. Let me introduce my new friend, Thomas." Mr. Hyatt and Thomas shook hands. "Thomas and I are getting to know each other."

Mr. Hyatt interjected, "Why don't he and I get to know each other while we do some work? You can go mingle and inspire the troops."

Brad laughed and turned to address Thomas. "You're okay, right?"

"Yes, it looks like I am in good hands. I'm sure we'll talk more later."

Mr. Hyatt and Thomas picked up trash together for a while in silence. Thomas asked, "So, what brings you out this morning?" Mr. Hyatt kept working as he replied, "Same as everyone else, I guess. Just trying to make a difference and give something back. You know, leave the world a little better than you found it."

Thomas probed further. "So, you're volunteering?"

Mr. Hyatt laughed. "Yes. Why, are you being forced to be here?"

Thomas looked in Brad's direction and paused before answering. "No, I'm here because I want to be. I was fortunate to get an opportunity and I'm glad to be here." He continued stuffing trash in a bag.

Mr. Hyatt delved further. "I noticed you looked at Brad before you answered; want to tell me about it? It looks like we'll be here a while."

Thomas beamed—this was his big chance. "How about if I start at the very beginning?"

Mr. Hyatt laughed. "That's always the best place to start a story."

The time flew by as Thomas told the story of his life—the truthful version—including how he met Brad. The park was beginning to take shape; it wouldn't be long before it was again enjoyed by children of all ages.

A young woman approached the men with bottles of cold water. Mr. Hyatt took two and passed one to Thomas. "Ready for a break?"

Thomas smacked his lips. "Don't mind if I do." He unscrewed the top, took a few swallows, and poured a little on the back of his neck.

Mr. Hyatt held his bottle up as if to toast Thomas. "You know, it isn't easy to put yourself on the line and tell a complete stranger your past. But, if a person will accept you at your worst, then there's nowhere to go but up."

"So, you saying you accept me?"

"Sure, why not?" Mr. Hyatt declared. "You're here working side by side with me, trying to make the world a better place. Why wouldn't I accept you? Because of something you did in the past? Looks to me like you're here making up for those mistakes, so I'd rather focus on the future—wouldn't you?"

Thomas grinned. "Yes, and thanks for being so understanding." The two finished their water and continued working and talking.

"What kind of future do you wish for?" Mr. Hyatt asked after a while.

"I want to be a great salesman!" Thomas replied confidently. It's what I love to do. But I'm not really sure how good I can be now if I'm going to use this new honesty plan. I mean, every one of the salesmen I know who are making a lot of money are dishonest. They aren't telling anyone the truth about their past and they pretty much lie every time they open their mouth."

Mr. Hyatt shook his head. "So you think you can't be successful telling the truth?" He turned and shouted across the park to another volunteer. "Hey Lonnie, can you come over here?"

A small man with salt-and-pepper hair, a bounce in his step, and a huge smile on his face came over. "Lonnie, this is Thomas. He's struggling with something and I think you can help."

Lonnie shook Thomas's hand. "Okay, hit me with it."

"Thomas doesn't fully believe that a person can be successful in sales by being totally honest. What do you think?"

Lonnie couldn't wait to reply, looking at Thomas sternly as he spoke. "I think you are dead wrong. There's a half dozen millionaires working here in the park who made their money in sales and are the most honest people you will ever meet." Thomas looked around in disbelief as Lonnie and Mr. Hyatt nodded in agreement. "Honesty will help you become your most Sensational Self, and the world will open up to you like a flower to the sunlight."

Brad came sauntering up. "What's the problem?"

Lonnie answered, "Your young newbie wants to be a salesman, but doesn't think he can make a good living by always telling the truth."

"So what did you tell him?" Brad quipped.

"That he was wrong," said Lonnie vigorously.

Mr. Hyatt added, "So, you told him at some point that honesty and integrity are the foundations for a sensational life. But, since he's never really lived that way, he doesn't fully believe it yet or know where to go from here."

Brad turned to Thomas. "So, you want not only to be an honest man, but to learn how to use that to your benefit and become a well-paid salesman?"

"Not in a greedy way," Thomas said quickly. "But I'd love to learn and I think I can be successful in sales!"

Brad looked Thomas up with affection. "So, you're telling me the guy I met last night, who's life was in the toilet, now has hope and wants to turn it all around?" He turned to Mr. Hyatt. "You've spent some time with him this morning—what do you think?" Thomas gave the older man a hopeful look.

Mr. Hyatt replied, "Well, I think only time will tell if he makes a true change in his life."

Lonnie looked at Thomas and chimed in, "I don't think you really understand the opportunity you may be getting here in this little park rehabilitation project. Do you realize you are surrounded by some of the smartest, kindest, and most selfless businesspeople you will ever meet? Not to mention some of my closest friends." He took a deep breath. "It can't just be about making more money."

"It's definitely not just about the money," Thomas said seriously. "I want the kind of life I've seen other people have." He looked at Brad. "The kind of life you seem to have. And now that I know where you came from, I see it's possible. But I just don't know how to do it." The other men raised their eyebrows in approval. "I'm willing to learn, and I know that being honest means I must be straightforward and stick to the facts. I also understand that having a high level of integrity means I must adhere completely and undividedly to a strict moral code."

"Well, he's starting out right," Lonnie observed.

Mr. Hyatt stepped in. "This isn't about memorizing a few definitions; it's about living your life as an example for others to follow. That's why we are all here today, because we choose to be the best people we can be every day—not just when it's easy or money is involved. Who you are is about what you do. Your actions will create the legacy you leave."

There was a long silence as the three men stared at Thomas for what seemed an eternity. Then he said, "I understand. I am willing to do whatever it takes to change my life for the better. If you will give me a chance, I'll prove to you I'm worthy. I'll make you all very proud of me."

"It's not about being worthy, or being validated by someone else," Brad said. "And don't do it to make us proud—you need to do it for yourself. The funny thing is, you can change if you really want to; if not, that old life of yours will be waiting patiently for you to return."

"It always is," Lonnie added with a laugh.

Brad cleared his throat and continued. "You see, Thomas, being honest and having integrity gives you the freedom to focus on other, more important things in life. It lets people know where you stand—and I'm not just talking about being a salesman. I mean in every aspect of your life. With honesty and integrity comes trust, and every meaningful, long-lasting relationship you will have in your life will boil down to trust."

Thomas replied quietly, "I want to be trusted again. Even if I don't make it as a salesman."

"Sounds like the man really wants to make a change," Mr. Hyatt observed.

Lonnie agreed. "Sounds sincere, but only time will tell."

"Okay, let's wrap this project up and then we can discuss the possibility of a next step," Brad concluded.

The volunteers gathered again. Thomas looked back one last time at the park. He was astonished at how it had transformed throughout the day—from a disaster to a place beautiful and ready to be enjoyed. Lonnie, Mr. Hyatt, and Brad were conversing and periodically looked over in Thomas's direction. When Thomas finished loading trash bags into a dumpster, he walked over to join them.

Brad greeted him. "So, I'm betting the day probably turned out much differently than you were expecting."

Thomas grinned. "I didn't know what to expect, but I never thought I'd be spending the day cleaning up an inner-city park."

"Doesn't it feel good to know your efforts are going to make a positive difference in people's lives?" Mr. Hyatt added.

"Definitely!"

Lonnie patted Thomas on the back. "So, will we be seeing you again?"

Thomas looked at Brad and said, "I hope so, if you'll have me. I'll come running with an extra set of hands the next time I'm asked."

"And what about you becoming a top dog salesman?" Mr. Hyatt asked. "What's your plan for that?"

Thomas faltered a bit. "I'm—not really sure. But I know it's what I want."

"What would you think about working with me to become that great salesman?" Brad said.

Before Thomas could respond, Lonnie blurted out, "Before you answer, you need to realize the magnitude of what Brad's saying. I gotta believe that if you give the same kind of effort as you did today, there's no limit to what you may achieve with him as a mentor."

Thomas looked around at the smiling faces of the volunteers, whose laughter filled the air. Even after a full, hard day of work, everyone seemed so happy. He addressed Mr. Hyatt. "So, you're all here because of Brad?"

"No, we are here because we believe in giving back. But our lives were all changed thanks to him, and I know if you take full advantage of any opportunity he may offer you, your life will no doubt be changed for the better."

Thomas looked at Brad and said sincerely, "As I said earlier, I really want to have a better life. And I know I need help to get there. I'd be honored to be around you more. I want what everyone here seems to have, and it looks like you might be the answer. So—I'd say yes to whatever you have in mind."

Brad smiled. "Well, I don't know about being the answer, but we have had a great deal of success helping other people achieve their goals. I'd like to see you do the same. I have a few sales positions I'm looking to fill, but I won't hire just anyone to join our team. I look for special people who I'm convinced will learn our system and commit one hundred percent. We have had great success with our method, but finding the right people isn't always easy."

"So, you think I have what it takes?" Thomas said.

Lonnie spoke for Brad. "From what I've seen today, you may have what it takes. Brad asked us about it and we all think that you'd probably do well, but it's a long process and there's no room for half-stepping."

"You've already started the transformation," Mr. Hyatt added. "You were honest with me and spent your entire day helping others. I think you're ready."

Brad addressed Thomas. "How about we call it a day and I take you home?

"That sounds great," Thomas exhaled. The two men said their goodbyes and headed to the car. Thomas walked with a lively step, his head held high, his shoulders back, with a confident grin on his face. They got in the car and buckled up for the ride home.

Brad turned to Thomas and said, "I appreciate your help today. As I said before, I believe everything happens for a reason. It looks like our meeting wasn't a coincidence."

"Definitely not a coincidence," Thomas agreed. "Weird to say, but I am happy you splashed me—otherwise who knows where I'd be right now."

To Brad, Thomas appeared hopeful, energetic, and entirely different from the man who had climbed into the car the night before. "First, I need to hear it all, your entire life story, and don't leave anything out."

Thomas laughed. "I know, I know, start at the beginning, be totally honest—and don't worry, I won't leave anything out. I did this earlier with Mr. Hyatt." He began to tell his story as Brad drove. Just about the time they pulled up to his house, he finished his story. "So, here we are. Now what's going to happen?"

Brad turned the engine off. "You need to become the best YOU possible, and being a good salesman will follow. No question you have potential, but there's still a great deal for you to learn. Every person we hire goes through the same basic training program regardless of what position they are going to fill. They work with several mentors and learn all the important lessons before we place them in one of my companies. If they listen, learn, and apply what we teach, they always rise to the top. So, here's what happens next. You will begin on Monday. I bet it will be unlike anything you have experienced before. The schedule will vary. During the training phase, it won't be your typical nine-to-five job, so you'll have to be flexible. Some days you will have an assignment that only lasts a few hours; others days it will last from morning until night."

Thomas nodded in agreement.

Brad started the car up and continued, "Each one of the people I select for you to work with will teach the lessons I feel are important—the ones you must know. These are people I respect highly, so no matter what they ask you to do, please follow their instructions. Every one of them will play a part in your success, and perhaps someday it will be your turn to give back. I'm quite sure that at the end of each workday you will be ahead of where you started.

Although you may not see me every day, I'll be getting updates." He stuck out his hand to shake. "So, any other questions?"

Thomas shook hands. "I guess not."

"So, Monday at eight in the morning, someone will come and pick you up."

Thomas got out of the car. "I don't know if I will ever be able to repay you for this."

Brad smiled warmly. "I'm not expecting you to. This opportunity is a gift with no strings attached and no expectation of repayment. What you do with it is up to you."

Thomas nodded. "Well, until Monday, then."

He closed the car door and walked toward his house, stopping to pinch himself making sure he wasn't dreaming. He entered the house wearing a huge smile.

CHAPTER 3

Aim above morality. Be not simply good, be good for something.

—Henry David Thoreau

Values and Beliefs—What Do You Stand For?

As Thomas finished brushing his teeth, the doorbell rang. Just as Brad had said, it was eight o'clock and someone was there to pick him up. As he opened the door, a well-dressed chauffeur greeted him with a huge smile and a firm handshake.

"Good morning, Mr. Frickle. Hope you are well rested and ready for a Sensational day."

For the first time in as long as Thomas could remember, he felt respected and important. He was eager and filled with energy to begin his new adventure. He hesitated for a split second wondering what the day would bring, then grabbed a jacket and headed out.

The chauffeur opened the door to the limousine and Thomas climbed in. He was surprised to find he wasn't alone. Across from him sat a man who was talking on a cell phone. He smiled and raised one finger as if to say he would be off in a moment. Thomas sat quietly looking the man over as the car began to move. He was probably in his forties, well groomed, sharply dressed, and had a soothing voice. Finally, the man's call came to an end.

"Good Morning, Thomas. My name is Victor Hall. I'm excited that we are going to spend the day together." They shook hands and the car took off smoothly.

The two men chatted during the thirty-minute drive. The car came to a stop and the chauffeur opened the door. As the two men exited, Thomas realized they were at the entrance to the zoo and botanical gardens.

The chauffeur handed both men umbrellas and said, "Here you are, gentlemen. I will be back to pick you up at three thirty." He handed Victor a business card and continued, "I'm sure you already have it in your phone, but just in case, my cell number is on here if you need me sooner."

With a tip of his hat, he was back in the car and on his way. A light rain began to fall. The two men opened their umbrellas and headed toward the entrance.

Thomas had thought several times about bringing Sandy here on a date, but never got around to it. He looked at the empty parking lot. "Are you sure they are open—you know, with the weather and all?"

Mr. Hall replied, "It's open, though some of the animals won't be out due to the rain. But my favorite exhibits are inside anyway, so we should be just fine."

Thomas was a bit nervous since Brad hadn't given him any idea of what was to take place. He figured it was as good a way to spend the day as any other, but since he didn't have a job now and needed a new source of income fast, he hoped to learn something that would help the situation. It seemed a little unorthodox, but he wasn't about to question things. Mr. Hall paid for both men and they entered the zoo.

After a few minutes of walking silently, the two men stopped in front of a large pen that housed two giraffes. They were enjoying the slight drizzle as they snacked on leaves from the tops of the trees.

Victor began speaking. "Thomas, I've worked for Brad for several years. My role is to determine if you have what it takes to join one of his companies." Victor looked Thomas over from head to toe with an evaluating glare. "I like to get to know someone personally. Although you and Brad have spoken on a few occasions, it's my responsibility to thoroughly interview you and report my findings." They continued walking, mindful of the puddles.

"Brad brings me potential candidates all the time. He finds them in all kinds of places, as he did you. If he gets a feeling they may have something positive to offer, he starts the process by sending them to me. I check their background and spend the day with them, just like we are doing now. We do this before investing a great deal of time, money, and energy in someone who doesn't match our core requirements, or have the willingness to change. It's my job to see if you have what it takes to become a good fit. I am the judge and I fulfill that role very well."

Thomas nodded amenably. "I understand."

Victor continued, "If today goes well, then there'll be a tomorrow. You'll meet with a new person who will build on what has already been discussed and agreed upon by you, Brad, and myself. Each day's new instructor will address a new topic that we feel is vital for any successful person to know. These trainers are hand-picked because of specific knowledge they possess. They each have an area of expertise we feel is crucial to a person's initial training."

Thomas interrupted, "So how long will it take?" The rain began to come down with force, causing the men to seek shelter. They entered the reptile building and shook the water from their umbrellas.

Victor answered, "The initial training usually takes a couple of weeks if everyone's schedules work out."

Thomas wondered why they were in a zoo rather than a corporate office, but he was too intimidated to ask. He had to keep the faith and knew this was better than any other prospects he had. While staring at a snake display, he remembered his high school history class and the story of Cortez. When Cortez was discovering new lands, he would arrive on shore and have his men burn their ships. Thomas knew that was the kind of commitment he needed now.

Victor cleared his throat. "Let me ask you—what do you believe?"

Thomas looked stunned for a second and then stuttered, "Believe—believe about what? The question took him by surprise and he was now concerned about impressing the man.

Victor spoke again, "For instance, do you believe you're a good salesman? Is life fair? Was your recent firing justified?"

Thomas said, "How long do we have?"

Victor smiled. "As long as it takes for me to get an understanding of who I am really working with. Since you already learned the first lesson from Brad, I'm sure honesty won't be a problem."

Thomas shook his head. "No, not at all. I've learned how important that really is—which I guess I could say has already affected my beliefs."

Victor raised an eyebrow. "Explain what you mean."

While the two men spent the next hour walking around the zoo, Thomas bubbled as he explained how he had already changed since meeting Brad. Victor asked pointed questions to uncover Thomas's genuine core beliefs. The two men stopped at the lion exhibit.

Victor said, "I am glad you are being so open with me. Sometimes people are afraid to share what their true beliefs are."

Thomas replied, "After meeting Brad, I have a different outlook on sharing myself. I am definitely not as fearful as I was a few days ago."

Victor said, "You probably remember this from when you were a kid, but at one time everyone in the world thought the earth was flat?" Thomas nodded in agreement and thought, *And I was just thinking about Cortez.* Victor continued, "And then someone proved it wasn't flat. It took courage and a belief system that allowed them to question everything and discover new possibilities. Our company wants to hire people who believe all things are possible. Are you that kind of person?"

Thomas paused and then replied, "All things? Let me think for a moment."

Victor continued, "Well, while you are thinking, did you also know that at one time it was thought the earth was the center of the universe?"

Thomas quipped, "Yes, I remember studying that."

Victor chuckled. "Then you would have known that during the sixteenth century Copernicus and Galileo risked imprisonment and being burned at the stake to change our beliefs and put the sun at the center of the universe. But things didn't stop there, no, no, no. Along comes a man named Edwin Hubble in the 1920s who shows us the sun isn't the center of the universe. My point is, your beliefs need to be your own and you need to arrive at them through effort, investigation, and education."

Thomas wanted to show his wit and contribute something tangible to the conversation. "Then you would agree that we can have common beliefs, such as doing good is always better than doing bad? Or People deserve a second chance."

Victor replied, "Common beliefs are why we are together today. We won't believe exactly the same thing if we look at a thousand specific examples. But our core beliefs: those need to match in order for you to be successful with us. It isn't uncommon for companies to administer a battery of tests to determine a person's beliefs before they will offer you a position. They may also conduct personality examinations. I would rather do the testing myself." He released a knowing smile. "I have been called the human lie detector, the brain doctor, and many things much less flattering. But my background as a CIA agent specializing in interrogation has given me a specific set of skills that come in handy when trying to get to the core of who someone is."

Thomas was visibly shaken and stepped back. Victor said calmly, "Not to worry, you are doing fine."

Thomas spoke, "But what if I have something strange or quirky about me that you or Brad don't find acceptable?"

Victor stepped forward and put a consoling hand on Thomas's shoulder. "Don't panic just yet."

Thomas replied, "But now you've got me thinking. Before today I never gave my core beliefs any thought. If I don't have what you and Brad are looking for, I'm out of luck."

Victor chuckled and shook his head as they began walking from the zoo toward the botanical gardens. He continued, "Don't worry, you seem pretty lucky. Unfortunately, many people are afraid to find out what they truly believe. They spend all their lives with self-imposed limiting beliefs. The good news is your beliefs can be changed in a just a few minutes."

Thomas looked excited, "Really?"

Victor continued, "Really, if one understands a few basic principles, a person can change their beliefs pretty easily. Your beliefs were programmed mainly by accident, over the course of a lifetime. Many times the change is a result of being hit by a traumatic or significant emotional event. Other times it's by being exposed to something new or by stepping out of your comfort zone."

Victor continued, "There are various ways someone might identify and change what they believe. I'll give you an example. Before 1954, running a mile in under four minutes was thought to be humanly impossible. There were theories that runners would simply drop dead. Then, in a few short minutes, a man named Roger Bannister changed what everyone believed and broke the record. The repercussions were huge. The next year, over thirty people accomplished the same feat. Each year since, more and more people join that sub-four-minute-mile club. You see, I didn't have to accomplish a thing to change my beliefs. I only needed to witness it." Thomas gave an understanding nod.

The two gentlemen entered the botanical garden and Victor continued, "So, the reason these things are important to Brad is he knows that to be a good salesman, you need to understand not only your own beliefs, but the beliefs of your current and potential clients. When you are trying to build a relationship with someone, it will be imperative you know the point they are starting from and whether you have common beliefs. If you are strictly a follower and never do any original investigating or thinking for yourself, what are the odds you will ever help someone change their beliefs?" Victor stopped to enjoy a bronze replica of *The Thinker*, by Rodin. After a few contemplative moments, he broke the silence, "You may be thinking, why do I want to change their beliefs?"

Thomas said, "Does it have to do with brainwashing?"

Victor laughed. "Don't let my background confuse you. Not brainwashing, and I'm not talking about coercion or manipulation either. Notice, I also didn't say selling them, closing them, or conning them. I'm talking about bringing a person from a place where they don't see the possibility of something to a place where it is possible or attainable. Remember, beliefs are at our core and most people are guarded, so their beliefs won't be easily accessible. Most people fear changing who they are or what they think. But the beauty of understanding this topic is that you can help people by identifying and changing the beliefs that keep them from getting what they want and from achieving the success they desire. I'm talking about overcoming limiting beliefs." With a wink and a nod, Victor seemed totally overjoyed with the prospect of helping others.

They continued walking as the rain came to a halt and the sun began to peek from behind the clouds. The two were interrupted when a man began loudly chastising his child for dropping an ice cream cone on the ground. Thomas shook his head and they continued walking until they found a bench, wiped the water from the seat, and sat down.

Victor began, "Observing those you are with and learning about their beliefs will help you become a better communicator and develop long-lasting relationships. For instance, here's an obvious observation I made of you while in the zoo. You are probably not an animal rights activist. The entire time we were at the zoo, you were content to view the animals through the bars of their confined habitat. You didn't mention how cruel it was, or show a bit of sadness regarding the animals. Now, I am not saying that is a good or bad thing. But if you had a deep belief or conviction about it, you probably would have shown signs I would have recognized."

Thomas replied, "That makes sense. I can see how that information could help in certain situations."

Victor continued, "Even small bits of information you gain about a person's beliefs can help you create a total picture." He located the father and child and pointed them out. "But what I also noticed is how you reacted when that man scolded his child for dropping the ice cream cone. You seemed to lose your focus and had a look of pain on your face when it happened. You glanced back several times and I truly thought you were going to intervene."

Thomas seemed sickened by the episode. "I wanted to say something. A zoo trip with a father is supposed to be the greatest day ever, but kids will make mistakes and accidents will happen. It was just a little ice cream cone, not the end of the world."

Victor replied, "So think about how you differentiate between animals and children. More important, how do you think that child's belief system will be affected after an experience like he had today?"

The two men rose and began to walk again. Victor spoke softly, "We learn our beliefs by what we see and experience. So how you were treated as a child, how you were spoken to, whom you were raised around, and what you were taught had a huge impact on the core beliefs that are now deep inside you. Then, as we grow and live, we continue to evaluate and adjust our beliefs. The problem is, most people are doing it subconsciously and letting other people program them. We are the sum of our experiences. So let's look at you as a sales professional for a minute. Have you been to any sales seminars or classes?"

Thomas answered eagerly, "Yes, several very good ones and a couple of bad ones."

Victor continued probing. "I would guess that in most of the courses you were taught that customers are to be persuaded, manipulated, and closed? Well, if you believe that is the definition of sales, because that's what you experienced and were taught, then I would expect you to do those very things when put in front of a customer. You believe it's the right thing, because that's what you know. Just as people thought the earth was flat."

Thomas gave an agreeable grin and nod of his head. "So I need to relearn some beliefs and I may need to help my customers or potential customers change some of theirs? But what if I'm not right?"

"It's up to the customer to determine what's right for them; your job is simply to provide options and to fill a need." Victor added, "You will need to become an active listener to understand what starting point people are at with their beliefs and what information you should provide to truly help them acquire what they want and need."

Thomas laughed. "It sounds like I need to be a counselor."

Victor chuckled. "I guess if you want to become a sensational salesman, you do need to do some counseling. We provide our people with a different set of tools in order to be successful. It's not your typical, routine sales pitch method—"

"What other ways are there?" Thomas interrupted.

Victor looked satisfied with Thomas's question and patted him on the back. "I'm glad you are interested—that's a great sign. So, first, let's get a handle on the dictionary definition of a customer. Before I begin, I need to quench my thirst." They stopped at a vending machine and got a couple of drinks.

Victor took a long drink from his bottle and continued. "By definition, *A Customer is one who receives (purchases, in most cases) a commodity or service.* Do you believe that to be true?"

Thomas swallowed deeply and said, "Yes that sounds right."

"Do you also believe that if we don't have customers, we don't have a business?"

Thomas nodded. "That makes sense, but it doesn't sound any different from what everyone else teaches."

"That's true," Victor agreed. "Most people don't begin to diverge on their beliefs until this point. Do you believe the customer is always right?"

Thomas took a little longer to respond. "Well, I've worked for some companies that said yes and said some that said no."

Victor pressed sternly. "So which do you believe?"

Thomas knew this was an important answer. "I guess—I guess I don't have a set belief."

"Well, you probably do have a belief, but it just may not be that strong. It isn't a deep conviction, so we could educate you to adopt our beliefs regarding customers."

Victor began to be more enthusiastic as he continued, "We feel we have a belief that allows you to work both sides of the equation. We believe that the customer is not always right, *but*—you don't have a business without customers."

Thomas chuckled. "That almost sounds like you are dodging the subject a little bit."

Victor quickly replied, "That's one way to look at it, but we would like to think we have come up with a belief that allows our people to respond to both the needs of the customer and the company equally. Many people who join our staff don't come to us with that belief, but they begin to change when they see things work out positively. Kind of like those people who found out the earth wasn't flat: it was a whole new reality to accept, and once that happens, you never consider the original one again.

The two men came to a halt staring into a sea of tulips. Victor turned to Thomas. "Now, do you realize the connection between your beliefs and what you value?

Thomas replied, "Honestly, I kind of thought they were the same thing?"

Victor continued, "They are definitely different. Think about something you value, something you wouldn't want to lose or that you would put a high price tag on." He bent to smell the flowers and waited for the answer. "I'm going to pick on you for a second, but I'm sure you can take it. It may be an oversimplification, but I would bet you didn't value honesty in the past. I mean, really cared deeply and cherished it." He raised his eyebrows, waiting for Thomas to respond.

Thomas sighed. "And you would have been right before I met Brad. I didn't hold honesty dearly and I'm now fully understanding the cost of not valuing it more."

Victor said gently, "Let's hope you find it priceless from now on, because everyone in our organization does, and we defend it with everything we have." He turned and walked ahead as Thomas hustled to catch up. Thomas felt a deep sense of guilt and regret for all the lying he had done for much of his life. Looking back, he had gained nothing of value by lying, but it had cost him a fortune of happiness as well as his income.

"We have to be careful," Victor continued slowly. "People can change overnight, though they usually don't. It was just a couple of days ago that you were hurting all the people around you, especially those who deeply cared for you. As humans, everything we do is for one of two reasons: either to avoid pain or to gain pleasure. So, if you valued honesty and it created great pleasure to be honest, and caused you great pain when you got caught lying, you wouldn't give the truth up for any price. It would be too painful to be dishonest. Does that make sense?"

Thomas nodded in agreement. "And if a person falls into the trap of lying to himself to keep from dealing with something that is extremely painful, then they probably won't value honesty. Their pleasure will come from escaping the reality."

Victor stopped again, staring out at the field of tulips. "Did you know that at one time in history, tulips were more valuable than gold or silver?"

Thomas was intrigued. "I can't say that I have ever heard that."

Victor reached down to smell a flower. "That seems ludicrous now, but it's true. The fact is, most people value the wrong things. They care too much about material things. And like those tulips, the

36

value can change in an instant." He shook his head in disgust. "In reality, *people* are the most valuable items on the face of the earth, and that's a belief we hold dearly." He moved on down the path. "Of course, value is all about perception, and perceptions change like the wind." He watched as the flowers swayed in the breeze. "Look at precious metals, or how a new car depreciates the minute you drive it off the lot, or the almighty dollar: those values are in a constant state of change."

Thomas was totally engaged now. "I guess I would agree that people hold the highest value."

Victor stopped. "You guess? That means you are torn. It means your belief system isn't set on this topic yet. So what are the most valuable items on the face of the earth?" He began to wave his hands. "Most people would respond with gold, diamonds, or even oil. The truth is, without humans to put a value on those things, they are worthless. Have you ever seen an animal trading gold, wearing a diamond, or using oil? Didn't think so. Humans are the greatest miracle. They have the most potential, and therefore the highest value to our organization—at least that's what we believe."

The two men walked toward the exit. Victor continued, "So, who can take natural resources, raw materials, or an idea and make something of it? The intangible aspects of a person, like their heart, determination, creativity, imagination, and a long list of other attributes, are why we believe our team members are the most valuable assets in our company. But if a person believes that their happiness comes from material things and people bring them pain, then their belief system will be in contrast with ours. To add to that idea, we also believe people have different values. If you were on a deserted island with six people and one was a doctor and the other five needed surgery to live, who do you feel is most valuable at the time?"

"The doctor would be most important for sure."

"But remember, I said the value of people can change quickly. Let's take the same deserted island, but no one needs surgery, and the doctor was the only one who didn't have the skills to start a fire, hunt, fish, collect water, or build a shelter. Do you think he would still be the most valuable?"

Thomas joked, "I think he would be voted off the island."

Victor chuckled. "So, hopefully you see why we believe a person who is versatile, adaptable, and has the willingness to evolve is the kind of team member who will help us continue our success. If everything works out and you complete the entire course of study with us, you'll be introduced to many different ways of doing things. You may already believe you are proficient in those areas. A lot of people think they know it all. But, regarding you specifically, if you were successful using your own methods and beliefs, then how did you ruin your life so totally and completely?"

Thomas dropped his head, feeling a little embarrassed as Victor hammered the point home.

"Remember, we value honesty, and that should be easy to make a habit, since you understand firsthand how much pain the lack of it can bring you and those around you." He put a fatherly arm around Thomas to console him. "I'm sorry if my words hurt you, but in time you'll heal."

The two stopped and Victor looked Thomas deep in the eyes. "If you want to be responsible for your own growth, don't wait for anyone else," he said solemnly. "Start working on it immediately. Nourish your mind with good books and feed your soul with information that will enable you to be successful. There are libraries full of great books, and more information on the Internet than you could ever digest in a lifetime. I can get you books that will help you understand belief systems and what motivates people to behave the way they do. But, just like any other resource, it will only help if you apply yourself."

Thomas replied softly, "I want to be the best person I can be. I want to learn the right things, and never go back to my old life."

Victor smiled with approval. "It's painful looking back, isn't it?"

Arriving at the exit, Victor whispered, "If you decide to go to work on yourself, on what you truly believe and value, you'll start by asking lots of tough questions. More important, you'll need to answer them honestly. Self-discovery is an incredibly liberating exercise. You've already spent a good portion of your life trying to convince other people to buy into your beliefs." He tapped his head. "Your parents did it to you constantly as you were growing up. It's a cycle."

He continued, "Think about it, how many of your current beliefs did you really establish on your own? Through education or exposure, you may have changed some of your original beliefs. To truly know, when you start your discovery, ask yourself questions like Why am I at my present job, or on my current career path, and What do I believe about my last company, my departure, or my ability to help others? Ask about what your capacity to learn is, to be wealthy, or to have a long life. Ask if you believe people can be rehabilitated, whether there is a God, or if all men are created equal. It doesn't matter what you ask, what you want to know is whether the answers are truly your own beliefs, or someone else's you adopted without any thought. Most people will find they never actively created their own belief system through conscious investigation, education, and analysis."

Thomas interrupted him. "I get it and I can see the importance. If you really evaluate yourself, you will get clarity regarding whether you are living your life by your own rules, or someone else's."

Victor looked surprised. "That was well said. I think you are really getting it."

As the two men exited the park, they noticed the limo at the curb and the chauffeur waiting patiently. They climbed in and the driver pulled away.

Victor continued, "So, tomorrow you will be on your own during the day, and I'll be back to pick you up at seven in the evening for a very interesting experience." He picked up a bag and opened it for Thomas. It contained books, CDs, and DVDs. "This bag is full of tools and resources that we have found to be helpful to other people during the first phase of training. There's even a CD that will help you with the self-discovery exercise we talked about. I would like you to spend the entire day evaluating and studying who you are and what you believe."

Thomas nodded, "So, I'm on my own?"

"Yes, but if you have questions or if something comes up, you can always call me. We've found this process is really about you digging deep down inside yourself, and each person goes about it differently. Find a quiet place and spend time getting to know *you*!"

After a relaxing drive, they came to a stop in front of Thomas's house. He got out of the car.

"Can you think of anything else you may need?" Victor asked. With a long look at the bag, Thomas replied, "No, I think I have everything. Let's hope I can find all the answers in one day."

Victor laughed. "I'm not worried about you finding all the answers; in fact, you might not even figure out all the questions in one day. Don't panic—just get to work on yourself."

The two men shook hands and the driver closed the door. Thomas watched the car drive away and turned toward his house. As he headed to the door, he noticed several of his neighbors staring in his direction. With the bag under one arm, he waved proudly and said, "Good Evening." They returned the wave. Thomas smiled warmly to himself. He entered his house with a new sense of pride and confidence that made him truly feel like the king of his own castle.

CHAPTER 4

The single biggest problem in communication is the illusion that it has taken place.

—George Bernard Shaw

Communication—What Are You Really Saying?

The pile of paper at Thomas's feet was ankle deep as the sun set over his shoulder. He had spent the day sitting on his back porch filling pages of a yellow legal pad with everything he could think of regarding his beliefs. He discovered a number of limiting beliefs that had kept him from fulfilling his potential. He wrote down how he arrived at those beliefs and how he was going to change them. It was interesting to learn how his beliefs had been established. One thing was for sure, he didn't want to move forward in his new life until he understood everything and had created a master list and knew exactly where he stood when it came to his beliefs.

The outdoor landscaping lights automatically clicked on, which prompted Thomas to gather his books, papers, and CDs and head into the house. He laughed as he thought, *A completely full day and I never felt like I was working.* It was six thirty when he glanced at his watch. He still needed to shower and get dressed. He didn't know what might happen that night, but he was excited.

When his stomach growled, he realized he hadn't stopped to eat lunch—it was crazy how his schedule was evolving since meeting Brad on Friday night. But he was happy, because for the first time in as long as he could remember, he felt truly alive. He quickly grabbed a banana as he headed through the kitchen on his way to get ready.

Right on time, the chauffeur rang the bell and greeted Thomas as he opened the door. "Good evening, Mr. Thomas, I take it you are ready?" With a huge smile and a lively step, he closed the door and replied, "I can't wait." They laughed and climbed into the car, and Thomas greeted Victor as they quickly drove away.

After a long ride, they turned into the arts district, which was located at the edge of downtown. There was a large sign that read DIALOG IN THE DARK. Thomas had seen a special on the news about the attraction, but hadn't taken the time to visit. The exhibit allows people to spend a couple of hours experiencing what life would be like if you didn't have the ability to see. The car stopped at the curb and the chauffer let the two men out. They approached a window and Victor paid for their tickets. Entering the building, they found lockers to store their valuables; a worker provided each of them with a cane such as a blind person would use.

Victor asked Thomas, "So, can you define *communication?*"

Thomas replied, "Sure, it's when someone sends a message to another person or group of people." He nodded, trying hard to convince himself that he had the correct answer.

Victor continued, "That's close. Communication, by definition, is the act or process of using words, sounds, signs, or behaviors to express or exchange information, ideas, thoughts, and feelings."

Thomas agreed. "That's a lot better than my answer."

Victor continued, "Tonight we are going to build on what you have already been introduced to. So, let's make sure you are applying what you've learned so far. Do you believe that honesty is mandatory as you go forward in your life?"

"No question!" Thomas exclaimed quickly.

Victor nodded with approval. "Great—because it will make a difference in how you communicate with others and what you believe others are telling you. If you can't be honest, and that includes being honest with yourself, we believe it will be impossible to have successful communications with others."

Thomas added, "I *believe* that too."

The two rejoined the group and waited for their adventure to begin.

After a short time, a worker shuttled Victor, Thomas, and ten other visitors past a curtain partition and into a transition area, where they stood quietly. Within a few minutes a voice came over a sound system, asking each person to take a seat on one of the glowing cubes that were placed around the perimeter of the room. The voice continued, providing an explanation of what the guests could expect during the next couple of hours. The lights in the room slowly dimmed and a woman entered the room and introduced herself as Monica, their guide. You could only see her silhouette for a moment before the room was completely dark. She had a very calming voice and clear diction as she went around the room asking each person their name and where they were from.

Thomas thought, *If this is work, then it's the coolest job in the world.* The room became pitch black and you truly couldn't see your hand in front of your face. Thomas remembered Brad saying, "The most important part of being a good communicator is to listen." So, without visual cues, everyone in the group would have only the verbal directions the guide was providing and any other information that could be gleaned with their other senses.

Monica spoke, "Please make sure you follow in single file and stay in contact with the person in front of you. Use your cane rather than reaching out with your hands. There will be times when only the first few people will be able to hear my voice and my instructions, so you must listen and pass along the information appropriately." She led the group through a door: immediately it was as though they were in an outdoor park. Thomas could feel what seemed to be the sun on his face and hear birds chirping, dogs barking, and the wind rustling the leaves on the trees.

As they walked forward, he could feel the ground change from a pebbled path to grass and he could hear children playing in the distance. Monica asked everyone to move close to her and stop. She said, "Please tell me what you see."

Several people chuckled. A woman's voice spoke clearly, "I can't see anything—it's pitch black."

Monica spoke again: "You weren't always without sight, and though the surroundings are dark, if you use your mind's eye, you can see everything. Now, someone please tell me what you see."

A young man spoke excitedly, "I see several children playing tag and a dog running alongside them—"

Another man interrupted, "I see the leaves falling from the trees."

Monica interjected, "Much better. Once you understand that seeing isn't always done with your eyes, you will tap into something extraordinary within all of you. Now let's move on. Single file again, please." The group began to move.

As though struck by a lightning bolt, Thomas had an epiphany. He thought, *There is no doubt that communication is supremely important in business and you must make things perfectly clear to the people you are attempting to sell to. If you don't, they will fill in the blanks with what they already know and have seen in the past.* Although no one could see it, this revelation caused him to smile from ear to ear. *People will always enter a conversation with their own experiences in tow, or they will make it up on their own if you don't paint the picture properly.* Suddenly, he realized he had slowed a bit. Monica's voice had become faint and he couldn't touch the person he was supposed to be behind. Listening for any sound that would help him, he heard faint whispers. He zeroed in on the group and quickly caught up again.

Monica asked, "Are you truly hearing all the sounds around you?" as everyone moved through the park. Thomas could hear church bells—it sounded as if they were now near a busy metropolitan area. Each person moved to the edge of the park and stopped at what seemed to be a street with traffic. The noise increased and so did Thomas's stress level. Monica had them all draw close again and then asked, "How would you know when you should cross a street? What if no one is there to help you? What if a car decides to run a red light—how would you know?" She paused to let this thought sink in. "many of you walk down streets like this every day, not putting too much thought into anything around you. I don't have that luxury."

She turned and led the group safely across the street. She knew when to cross by the sounds of car brakes, the wind, and the different directions from which the noise of traffic came. In addition, she listened to the countdown beeps for the "Walk" light, which most people never notice because they are so visual.

As the tour continued, the group visited a grocery store, boarded a boat and took a ride around what seemed to be a lake, and then finished up in a bar where they ordered drinks. They followed Monica's voice all the way back to the glowing cubes where they began. As the room slowly filled with light, Monica spoke softly, "It has been a privilege to share this experience with you today. If you were wondering how we did this, I'm sorry, but I can't give away our secrets. I can tell you for sure that we didn't leave the building and you were never in harm's way." The lights came up fully. While everyone's eyes adjusted, she continued. "And yes, I am one hundred percent without sight and have been for ten years. But please don't feel bad, because I probably see more every day without the use of my eyes than most people with perfect vision ever do."

An appreciative murmur passed through the group. Monica continued, "Did you notice that there were times during our journey when you might have thought you were helping others in your group by giving information? But multiple people trying to solve a problem in the dark actually may have made things worse." Many of the group nodded in agreement. "For the most part, you moved in a straight line, so just as in the old game, Whisper Down the Lane, the message got passed from one person to the next. How many times did the details get lost when the instructions were retold? Some of the time it was easy—touch this, describe that, turn left, turn right, watch your step—but often life is much more complicated than that, wouldn't you agree?" Everyone nodded this time. "Now, please, raise your hands if you feel you have been drifting through life and taking your sight for granted." Everyone's hand went up.

A man said, "Now that I think about it, I can't believe how much I've missed out on in my life because I count on my eyes so much."

Monica laughed. "I would never want someone to be without sight; I just wish they could be more balanced and actively use all their senses. It leads to a richer, fuller life. Think about how many times your eyes can fool you." Her voice grew louder as she continued, "It's not just because I'm blind, but you can actually tune in to the world at a deeper level through what you hear. The tone of someone speaking, how they are breathing, the words they choose." She took a long pause. "I can say that since I have lived with sight and without, if I got to choose which sense I would lose, I would honestly rather it be my sight as opposed to my hearing."

The man said, "Wow—that's wild."

She continued, "Sure, there is sign language, but it doesn't cover all the nuances of sound. Plus, I'm an auditory learner, so I love to hear everything."

Monica moved to the exit and spoke one last time. "Please remember that poor communication can actually do more damage than no communication." She paused for effect. "I'll leave you with something my grandfather use to say. 'You were given two ears and one mouth for a reason: listen twice as much as you speak.'"

She opened the door to let the group out of the room. "I hope you have enjoyed yourselves and perhaps learned a little something along the way." The group began to file out. As they passed Monica, she smiled and gave each person a warm hug.

Thomas and Victor made their way to meet the car and climbed in for the ride home. Victor spoke, "So, very … eye-opening, wasn't it?"

Thomas said, "Yes, it sure makes you think."

Victor continued as the car pulled away, "We believe she is right: listening is the most important aspect of good communication. And if you get really good at it, you will be able to speak the language of whomever you are with instantly."

Thomas looked puzzled. "Are you saying I will be able to learn foreign languages?"

Victor laughed. "Not quite. I guess I should have gone over a few things before we headed out this evening. Did you hear Monica say she was an auditory learner?"

Thomas thought for a second. "Yeah, what did she mean?"

"Let me explain. There are three different learning styles: auditory, visual, and tactile. When people speak, they tend to use the language of their preferred style—the style in which they learn the best. Most people are dominant in one, but you might use all three fairly equally. Let me give you an example. Have you ever heard someone say, 'Do you see what I mean?' or 'I can't wrap my head around it'? or How about, 'Now, listen here'? These expressions give you an indication of the person's preferred learning style. If you can listen and figure that out, you can speak to them in their own language.

"For instance, I was in a meeting last week where the salesman kept saying, 'Do you see what I mean?' The only problem was, he was talking to an auditory learner. So, if he had really listened, he would have known the customer actually processes information better if spoken to clearly and with very specific words instead of being shown or painted a picture. So, *no*—the guy couldn't see what he meant.

"After what seemed to be an eternity, I stepped in and said, 'Please take a few minutes to clearly tell him all the features and specifications of the product.' The customer smiled and spoke up: 'Yes, please, I would love to *hear* every detail.'" Victor shook his head. "It sounds so simple—it's crazy more people don't acquire the skills."

Thomas said, "True, but they don't teach that in any school I ever went to."

Victor nodded in agreement. "I know. So when it comes to sales, can you *see* how much of an advantage you would have on the competition if you had those habits?"

Thomas laughed. "Oh, I get it. I'm a visual learner, so you said *see*."

"That's correct." Victor smiled. "Can you picture how well you will do when you fully understand it? There, I did it again. That's right—I didn't say, Let me tell you how good things are going to be, which would be auditory learning. Nor did I say, Let's roll up our sleeves and learn this today—"

"Which would be tactile," Thomas interrupted.

Victor sighed with delight. "That's right."

Victor tapped on the glass to get the driver's attention. "Please stop at that ice cream shop on the corner. I have a little more I want to share with Thomas, but I also have a bit of a sweet tooth."

The driver winked. "You bet."

"It may take another hour or so."

The driver smiled. "I'm here for however long you need me, sir."

Victor addressed Thomas again. "People get things wrong all the time, but having great listening skills will alleviate most mistakes and misunderstandings. And by the way, when I say great listening skills, I mean being an active listener. Do you know what that means?"

Thomas shook his head no. "I can try to guess, but would you mind explaining it to me, so I get it right?" He sat forward in his seat.

Victor replied, "Well, you are beginning to listen actively now, and you may not have realized it. You leaned forward, giving me all your attention. Being an active listener is about being engaged, and that's shown in a number of ways—"

"Should I grab something to write on?"

"You can, or just grab your smartphone and hit Record."

Thomas looked embarrassed "I had to turn that in when I got fired."

"No worries—although you are visual, just try listening for now, then."

The car came to a halt and the driver opened the door. "What can I get you two?"

Victor didn't hesitate. "Chocolate chip shake, extra thick." He turned to Thomas. "What are you having?"

Thomas thought for a second. "How about just a cup of chocolate almond."

Victor handed the driver cash, and the driver disappeared into the shop.

Victor continued. "Besides the physical act of turning your attention to someone, nodding in agreement, and making agreeable facial expressions, you can repeat back what you heard. Make sure to have patience and only do that at a natural breaking point in their speech. Don't be thinking about what you want to say while they are talking; truly listen, and then confirm a few items and points to reassure the other person that you are getting the message they are sending. Now, have you ever heard of NLP?" Thomas shook his head no. "It's an acronym for Neuro-Linguistic Programming. It's like having the combination to the safe of human behavior and communication."

"Sounds like something I'd definitely want," Thomas said.

"Earlier when I told you about the three learning styles, that's part of what you will learn," Victor continued. "But it's so much more than that. You'll also learn about nonverbal communication, which is incredibly important. In fact, most research states that it's more important than the actual words we use."

Thomas was listening with a huge smile on his face. "Well, I'll bet Monica might not agree."

Victor chuckled. "Perhaps, but take your smile, for instance. It shows warmth and acceptance, as long as it is an authentic smile—and we can tell whether it is by the muscles around your eyes."

Thomas made some funny faces, which caused Victor to laugh.

The driver opened the door and handed the two men their ice cream, "Here you go." Victor and Thomas replied, "Thank you very much." Both lit up like children and dug in with delight. Thomas swallowed, "I appreciate your paying for everything today."

"My pleasure. It is part of our investment in your training," Victor replied.

The two ate their ice cream in silence for a moment.

"We were talking about smiling," Victor continued. "Smiling changes everything. It provides a positive platform from which to start a conversation. I can pull into the driveway, see my wife at the front door, and know how she is feeling by the look on her face and how she is standing or moving. I can communicate how I'm feeling to her before I even get out of the car. Now, if either of us were without sight, that would definitely change the dynamic and make what I say and how I say it all the more important. If I make a sad face to her, she will immediately change moods, but if I smile—well, that changes everything." The two men leaned to the right as the car made a sharp turn and accelerated up the ramp to the highway.

Thomas asked, "So, is there more?"

Victor laughed. "More than you can learn in a night. It will take a while to see how things tie together—how people's communication is driven by those beliefs you've started learning about. Think about this: A dishonest person may give off signs that make others feel uncomfortable, even though his words might make perfect sense. Have you ever said to yourself, *I don't know what it is about that guy, I just don't trust him*? It may be that the nonverbal signs he is communicating don't match his words." Thomas nodded with understanding. "Let's not forget: there is intended and unintended communication. If I am sitting with one of my two sons, and I say that we should tell a little white lie to the other, I have now basically said that it is okay for him to lie as well."

The car began to exit the highway. Thomas spoke, "What a great evening. Will you thank Brad for me if you see him?"

"I definitely will," Victor answered with a chuckle. "Which brings up another aspect of communication—just to make your head swim. How do you handle sharing information through a messenger? How do you accurately relay someone else's message, or have yours sent the way you want it? What if something gets added, or left out? Many times what isn't said can communicate volumes, because the receiver was expecting a specific message or words. Why do you think there are so many marriage counselors in the world?" They both laughed.

Victor continued, "Tomorrow I would like you to do a few things on your own."

Thomas looked at him intently. "Okay, what are they?"

Victor counted on his fingers. "First, I have arranged for you to visit a sign language school. It's not so you can become fluent in sign language in a day; it's so you will look for aspects of communication that you never may have thought of. Second, I want you to go hang out at the mall." Thomas beamed from ear to ear. Victor shook his head. "No, not go shopping, but really hang out. Just like when you were a teenager."

"No problem," Thomas said.

"Let me explain, so you get the most out of the exercise. I'd like you to watch people as they communicate, but stay far enough away so you can't hear what they say. Try to figure out what they are saying by their body language, facial expressions, and gesticulations. Once you get good, you can usually tell at least what the main topic of the conversation is. Maybe a child is hungry, or a boyfriend wants to display public affection and the girl is uncomfortable, or maybe it's how mad one person is about how much money the other spent. The easiest ones to figure out are the bored spouses who are ready to go—yawning, looking at their watches, and rolling their eyes. Each of us has over 600 muscles in our face alone. That's where some of the best stuff really happens."

"I think I can handle those two things. Is that it?"

"No, there's one more thing." Victor grinned. "I'd like you to go home and watch a movie you've never seen, but you have to turn the sound all the way off. Then, after you are done, go back and watch it with the sound on." Thomas sat with a curious look on his face. Victor added, "See if you got what happens in the movie right. Those three things will give you a full day of work, and I think the exercises will help you become a better communicator. You see, your eyes can fool you, other people can confuse you, and words misspoken can lead you down the wrong path. Think about this statement: I shot an elephant in my pants. Without a picture, it takes a bit more explaining to fully understand, doesn't it?"

"There's so much more depth to everything now," Thomas exclaimed. "I just never looked at things the way I am beginning to. It almost feels like I have been in a coma and I'm just reawakening."

Victor raised his eyebrows. "Well said! Most people are missing out. They only have a couple of colors in their rainbow, or a few notes in their music. The goal is to be fully alive, and you definitely can't do that in a coma."

The two men had been in such a deep conversation they didn't even notice the car had already stopped at Thomas's home. Victor reached out his hand to shake. "You have fun tomorrow, and pay close attention. Brad will meet you tomorrow night. Oh, I almost forgot, when you first get to the mall, go by the tuxedo rental place—they are expecting you. They will give you something to wear tomorrow night."

As Thomas walked into the house and saw his reflection in the windowpane of the front door, anyone would have said that his face was a very happy one.

CHAPTER 5

If civilization is to survive, we must cultivate the science of human relationships—the ability of all peoples, of all kinds, to live together, in the same world at peace.

—Franklin D. Roosevelt

Relationships Are the Breath of Life

Thomas glanced in the mirror to straighten his bow tie. He could hardly believe he was wearing a tuxedo. Today had been interesting and he enjoyed the exercises, which allowed him to look at communication in a whole new way. As he was told, he started the day watching a movie, and then had the car take him to the sign language school and then on to the mall. He watched the movie a second time once he got home, spent time studying, and then spent the last hour getting ready. The doorbell rang at the expected time.

When Thomas opened the door, the driver said, "Let's get going—we will meet Brad there."

As the car pulled up in front of a restaurant, Thomas noticed a sign that read, HAPPY ANNIVERSARY TO THE SPENCERS. There was a long line of well-dressed people out the door and around the corner. Thomas exited the car and Brad greeted him. "Fancy meeting you here." The two men laughed and moved to stand in line with everyone else.

Brad began, "I'm glad you are here for this event. I hope you had a terrific day."

Thomas smiled. "It was amazing and I learned a lot."

"So, you probably want to know why we are both in these monkey suits. We are going to celebrate the wedding anniversary of two very dear friends, and you are going to be learning about relationships."

"Lord knows, I need to learn about those."

"The gentleman we're celebrating with this evening is a mentor and business partner of mine."

"I've been to anniversary parties, but never in a tux. So, these are pretty important people?"

"Important, for sure. These two lovebirds have the best marital relationship I have ever seen and, fortunately for you, they are willing to share some of their wisdom."

Thomas looked surprised. "Wow, on an important day like today? Why not some other time?"

"It's simple, you need the education. Anyway, Mr. Spencer insisted after I told him a little bit about you. So, relax and get ready to learn something about the things that matter most in life."

Within about twenty minutes, all the guests had entered and been seated. They made introductions and chatted with those at their table while waiting for the special couple to arrive. It seemed as though Brad knew everyone in the place. Finally, the elderly couple entered the restaurant to great fanfare, with help from a small band. Thomas was struck by how nimble they were for their age. They had to be in their late seventies but were holding hands and dancing arm in arm like two kids in puppy love. They made their way to the stage. It was sweet to see them dote over each other. Mr. Spencer carefully removed his wife's coat and pulled her chair out for her, showing her a high level of respect.

A man stepped up with a microphone, made introductions, and announced that the couple was here to celebrate their seventy-fifth wedding anniversary. The gentleman sitting next to Thomas said,

"Hard to believe she is ninety and he is ninety-one." He went on to explain that the couple had married young and then moved into a small one-bedroom house on his father's farm to help the family. They were also the proud parents of 11 children, all in attendance tonight. She had given birth to thirteen, but two had died. Back in those days, you needed a larger family to help with the farm chores and duties.

Brad turned to Thomas with a half-smile on his face. "It may seem like a party, but don't forget, this is also work." He broke into a chuckle. "This may be one of the most important days you have with us, so make sure you stay sharp." He glanced in the direction of the Spencers. "Grab a bite to eat, but don't go far; we are going to meet with Mr. Spencer in about fifteen minutes." Thomas gave an understanding nod and glanced at his watch. Brad got up and began shaking hands as he worked his way around the room.

Thomas made it to the buffet table and back to his seat with a plate of food. He ate quickly, knowing that Brad would be true to his word and return in just a few minutes. Thomas was watching everyone now, looking at how people were interacting and trying to guess what they were saying, even though he couldn't hear their conversations. He was really working at applying what he had been learning. He was also listening to the people at his table as they introduced themselves and told their own stories. Never once did he interrupt them or distract himself by worrying about what he wanted to say next. He made a point of turning his body and face toward those who were talking to him. There was no question he was becoming an active listener.

Right on time, Brad tapped Thomas on the shoulder and asked the table to excuse them. They headed up to the front of the room and stepped around the back of the stage. Brad got Mr. Spencer's attention. The elderly man turned, stood, and hugged Brad. "Brad, here to rescue me, my good man. Honey, look, it's Brad."

Mrs. Spencer turned and allowed Brad to kiss her on the forehead. "You are the only other man I would allow to kiss me."

She motioned to Mr. Spencer. "He was tired of this party before we ever got here. So do us all a favor and get him out of here for a few minutes." They all laughed.

Brad pulled Thomas forward and said, "I'd like to introduce you to the new friend I mentioned, Thomas Frickle."

Thomas shook their hands and said, "It is an honor to meet you both, and congratulations on your anniversary. It is quite an accomplishment."

Mrs. Spencer replied, "Thank you, young man. Now, please make sure you have my husband back here in time for the cutting of the cake." The three men reassured her and left the table.

They made their way to the kitchen, where they found a spot in the back corner by the walk-in. Brad began, "So, Thomas here has made a bit of a mess with some of his relationships. Most recently he lost the girl he loved and was set to marry."

Mr. Spencer looked disappointed. "Do you love her? I mean really love her?"

"More than anything," Thomas replied.

"Well, that might not be enough—it depends on how solid the account was before all this happened, and how big the check was that you bounced."

Thomas was confused. "I, I didn't bounce a check. I did a bunch of—"

"I don't mean literally. I'm talking about your relationship account."

Brad leaned in and said, "I hope you are paying attention, because he probably won't repeat himself."

Mr. Spencer closed his eyes and began to speak from the heart. "From now on, I'd like you to look at all your relationships as checking accounts. Do you understand how a checking account works?"

"Yes, I do."

"Good. Now, if you don't make any deposits in a checking account, and you write a check, what happens?"

"I guess it bounces."

The old man snapped, "You guess? Well, of course it bounces. So, the key to any good account, or any good relationship, is to make more deposits than withdrawals, and not only more, but bigger. That account must have a larger balance at any time than whatever withdrawal you intend to make. Does that make sense?"

"For sure," Thomas replied quickly.

Brad interjected, "If you were to look back, I would bet you have spent a lot of time being overdrawn on most of your accounts. Is that a fair statement?"

Thomas lowered his head. "Since I am being totally honest now, there's no doubt that's true."

Mr. Spencer continued, "Now, your deposits can earn interest, and if you don't make withdrawals, they will be compounded. Just like money, that's when real relationship wealth begins to take shape. Now, this is the part that I find most fascinating. If you are in healthy relationships, and you are making regular deposits, the other person will begin working just as hard to make deposits into your account. But don't get me wrong, this isn't a matter of *I'll do something for you so I can have something in return*. You do it without any expectation of something in return and because you love the other person enough to continue investing in them forever." He waited to allow this information to sink in for Thomas.

Mr. Spencer moved a little closer to ensure that Thomas was tuned in, since the noise in the kitchen seemed to increase. "So, now there will be two people contributing to that account. There will be so much money, even regular withdrawals won't hurt the balance. For instance, it's my seventy-fifth wedding anniversary and I am sitting in some kitchen, giving advice to a young man, with my wife sitting out in the dining room. Do you think this would have happened on my first wedding anniversary?"

Thomas made a distorted face. "I'm going to say no."

Mr. Spencer quipped, "You can say that again. But I am supported, because I've made a lot of deposits into this account and Brad has too. That's right: after a while, if you treat others well, people will line up to deposit into your accounts. But it all starts with you making those deposits, and not bouncing checks."

Brad said, "Think about it—this man is depositing into your account as we speak, and he doesn't even know whether it is still an open account."

Thomas said, "Everything you said is so simple and makes so much sense. And I can tell you are a very wealthy man when it comes to relationships. I've been learning how to listen, and I am going to take all of your advice to heart. Your deposit won't have been wasted on me. I can't thank you enough."

"Well, that's music to my ears," Mr. Spencer replied. He frowned. "Now, you need to bear in mind, tough situations will arise. For instance, I would never open an account with the intention of closing it, but it happens. Sometimes a relationship just isn't healthy. You realize that no matter how many deposits you make, the money is just being stolen. The person just leaves you high and dry. What you would rather have is an opportunity at least to leave that fortune stored up and perhaps someone you care about will be the beneficiary. Heck, I won't be here forever, but my banking history will—and that's why I am careful with every transaction. Because, my young friend, the most important lesson I can teach you is that true wealth will always be found in people. Invest in people and that is how you will become truly rich! Don't you think, when I'm gone, I'll have all these people to look out for my wife?"

Mr. Spencer looked at his watch and motioned that it was time to go cut the cake. Thomas stuck out his hand. "I am extremely grateful for the time you've spent with me, and I hope to be as wealthy as you someday—because of my relationships."

"Perhaps he is learning how to listen," Brad said, smiling.

Mr. Spencer said, "Before you leave tonight, you should have a word with my wife—believe it or not, she was the one who taught me this lesson. I learned everything I know about relationships from her, and she is the reason I am the happiest man on earth. Now let's get going before I bounce a big check." The three men laughed and headed back to the dining room.

The cake-cutting ceremony went smoothly. Then the couple danced alone under a spotlight, before everyone else joined in.

After a time, Thomas noticed that Mrs. Spencer happened to be sitting alone. As he walked over to speak with her, he reminded himself to be thankful, to listen actively, and to make a deposit.

Mrs. Spencer greeted him. "Did you enjoy yourself?"

"Yes, ma'am." He motioned to an empty chair. "Do you mind if I join you?"

"Please do," she replied, smiling.

"And did *you* enjoy yourself?"

Mrs. Spencer beamed with joy. "Most certainly." She seemed to be reminiscing, but he continued. "What your husband shared with me will definitely change my life." She turned and smiled, but still didn't speak. He leaned close to her and said, "Your husband told me that it was you who taught him everything he knows about relationships, and you are the reason he is a wealthy man."

Mrs. Spencer smiled even wider and said, "That's funny, because if I had spoken to you, I would have said the same things—I'd have said it was him. Perhaps that is why we are so happily married after seventy-five years, and the deposits just keep on coming."

Noticing Thomas sitting with Mrs. Spencer, Brad made his way over to them.

Mrs. Spencer said as he arrived, "It seems this young man is well on his way. Time will tell, and unfortunately we can't do it for him."

Brad nodded. "I think he will become wealthy indeed."

Mr. Spencer came up behind his wife and whispered something in her ear. She blushed, giggled like a schoolgirl, and said, "Well, gentlemen, it has been a true delight, but my husband has a very good idea of how we should end this evening, and it starts with us politely parting ways and heading for home." The foursome smiled, shook hands, and in the blink of an eye, the honored couple disappeared out the back of the restaurant.

Brad and Thomas decided to go outside and wind down in the nice weather. They noticed the limo parked close by and climbed up to sit on the trunk.

The driver opened his door. "I'm sorry I didn't see you come out. Are you ready to head home?"

"We're going to hang out here for a few minutes," Brad replied. "I want to cover a few more things, since I won't see Thomas for a few days."

"Not a problem, sir. Just let me know when you are ready." He closed his door and Brad turned his attention to Thomas.

"So, you do realize that at one time in my life, my accounts were all overdrawn and I was bouncing checks left and right?"

"Well, I know you shared how bad things were for you," Thomas replied. "So I can guess relationships were also a problem."

"It's really not as hard as people think," Brad continued. "If you want to have great relationships, you must give more than you get. It all starts with *you*!" Thomas nodded. "It was interesting—the more I did for the people I was already fairly close to, the more they did for me. I began to expand the practice to every person in my life." A sad look came across his face. "It really hit home with my wife. I had been doing such a disservice to her, expecting her to change, and expecting her to continue doing everything for me. My life was improving, I'd started being honest, staying out of trouble, but I hadn't figured out my relationship with her yet."

Brad was becoming more emotional as he spoke. "I bounced so many checks—it's hard to believe she didn't close down our account. Luckily, Mr. and Mrs. Spencer got hold of me, and I began to turn things around quickly. I did it for my wife, not because I wanted something in return. She deserved to be treated like a queen. I wanted her to be the most important aspect of my life, and that meant making whatever was important to her, important to me."

Brad grew quiet, and after a moment Thomas spoke. "Looking back, I probably did things for other people, hoping to get something in return. I'm overdrawn with everyone I know, including you."

"You can turn all that around," Brad replied. "Just stay focused, keep learning, and apply these lessons. Before you know it, you'll be wealthy beyond belief—I mean, look at me, for goodness sakes." He wiped his face on his hanky and became more focused. "You want to know when it got real interesting? When I began making deposits into my customers. Now, just as Mr. Spencer said, some accounts or relationships may not work out like you want. It's up to you to decide which relationships are going to be positive in your life. If you are investing and making deposits over and over again, and the other person is just taking withdrawals, you will have to evaluate whether that's a productive and positive relationship to keep. If it were a bank account, my guess is you would probably close it—right?"

Thomas nodded in agreement. "Just as Sandy did to ours."

"You've already learned about being honest. Well, great relationships have to have the same foundation. No matter what you think, honesty is always the most important part of a relationship, because that leads to trust. If you can't trust the person in the relationship, then it simply won't last. And to be trusted, you must trust."

"I hardly trust anyone," Thomas said ruefully, "because I know all the angles and think they must be trying to get something from me, just like I always did."

Brad continued, "Now, there's no doubt you will get some relationship scars. If you put yourself out there and invest or deposit in others, you'll get burned sooner or later. But scars can heal, and sometimes it's just not the right time for the relationship."

Thomas and Brad were startled by one of the cooks who slammed the side door to the restaurant as he was taking out the trash. Brad looked around and noticed the lights were off and the parking lot had emptied. He shook his head and said, "That's what happens, I just get carried away."

"I don't care how late it is," Thomas replied eagerly. "I'll stay here all night. I just want to be happy and get my life back in order.

61

I'd be a fool if I didn't take the time to learn from you and the Spencers. So, unless you have to go, I'll listen to anything else you are willing to share."

"Well, there are a few more things that I think are really important, and then we had better get us all home."

Brad stood with a purpose and began speaking quickly, as though he was now up against a clock. "It is your responsibility to lay the groundwork for the rules of your relationships. Didn't I do that with you?" Thomas nodded in agreement. "Don't be afraid to communicate your expectations and find out what the other person wants. I don't have unhealthy relationships, at least not for long. But I have to work on them all the time. Like most things in life, it is easier to be constantly working on a project than to let it get out of control and have to come back and do a huge renovation."

The two men were interrupted again as the rest of the restaurant staff exited the building, locked the door, and headed toward their cars.

"Think for a moment," Brad continued. "If you can build trusted business relationships, where the other person knows you are there to make deposits and help them fill their needs, don't you think you'll have a customer as long as the relationship stays healthy? You'll never have to sell them anything, because they'll always be asking to buy from you." Thomas gave an understanding nod and noticed Brad looking at his watch.

Brad put his hand on Thomas's shoulder. "Pretty long day, wasn't it?

Thomas leaned into Brad a bit and replied, "It was, but it was truly amazing. I mean, I'm going on sixteen hours and I don't feel one bit tired. A little overwhelmed, but not tired."

Brad gave him a fatherly pat. "It's a lot to soak in, but you are doing great. So go home, get some rest, and we'll keep marching on." He tapped on the window and the driver quickly bounded from the car and opened the rear door.

"Well, it is time to go. I had originally scheduled Victor to pick you up to meet someone at nine tomorrow morning, but I've already called and had it pushed back to one in the afternoon—that will give you both a chance to sleep in a bit." The driver flashed an appreciative smile.

Thomas shook Brad's hand. "I really don't mind getting up early. In fact, I'll probably be up anyway. The Driver wrinkled his forehead towards Thomas and he continued, "Or we can just keep it at one in the afternoon and let this gentleman catch up on some sleep, so he'll be wide awake while driving us tomorrow." Brad chuckled, "So, you are learning about non verbal communication." Thomas realized Brad had seen the interaction between he and the driver, "I'm definitely working on it." The men exchanged goodbyes and the driver took Thomas home.

CHAPTER 6

Life is not so short but that there is always time for courtesy.
—Ralph Waldo Emerson

Common Courtesy Isn't So Common Anymore

Thomas woke early and spent the entire morning filling his journal. Before he knew it, Victor was at the front door. They jumped in the car and after about a half hour of driving, Thomas began to notice all the storefront signs had changed to an Asian language. He remembered that this part of the city had a large population of Koreans. The car came to a halt at the entrance of a megastore, where Thomas and Victor got out. They entered the automated double doors and were quickly met by a man who was smartly dressed, had a flower in his lapel, and was wearing one of the biggest smiles Thomas had ever seen.

Victor stuck out his hand and greeted the gentleman. "How are you today, Mr. John?"

The gentleman shook hands with Victor and bowed his head at the same time. "I'm doing very well, Mr. Victor. Who is this you have brought with you?" They turned toward Thomas.

"Mr. John, this is Thomas Frickle, the young man Brad told you about."

Mr. John looked deep into Thomas's eyes and shook his hand with care and reverence. "It's my distinct pleasure to meet you, Thomas. I heard you had a late night, but I'm sure it was well worth it."

"The honor is mine," Thomas replied. "It was a late and great night, but I'm ready and excited to be here today. Thank you for adjusting your schedule. I know we were originally supposed to be here this morning." Victor raised his eyebrows, suggesting that Thomas impressed him with his interaction.

Motioning ahead of him, Mr. John said, "Why don't you follow me to my office." The men headed toward the back of the store, where Mr. John opened a door and allowed them to enter his office first. "May I offer you something to eat or drink?"

"No, thank you," said both visitors. Mr. John waited for Thomas and Victor to sit before he took his seat.

Victor spoke up, "Mr. John, I haven't shared today's topic with Thomas yet." Thomas sat forward with anticipation.

"Well, if you have made it here to me, then you already must have discussed honesty, your beliefs—oh, and communication and relationships."

Thomas smiled broadly. "That's exactly right."

Victor said, "Mr. John is very modest and would never say this to anyone, but he worked with Brad to develop our entire training system."

Mr. John seemed embarrassed. "I played a small role." He beamed and continued, "And I am blessed to present something that is dear to my heart." He said no more for a moment, bringing Thomas to the edge of his seat. "And that topic is common courtesy." Thomas sat for a second with his head cocked to one side, as though trying to let it sink in.

Victor added, "Just like each of the other topics you have been introduced to, common courtesy is a part of the foundation for every person who comes through the training. Unfortunately, many of the people we see hadn't previously made it an important aspect of their life. Not just their professional life—but their personal one." Victor paused. "And then they meet you!"

Mr. John smiled and continued, "Each trainer or mentor has their own strengths. We lead with what we're good at, but we never abandon the other aspects of our foundational training. I continue to improve in other areas—it's important to work on being well-rounded."

Victor rubbed his belly. "You know I'm succeeding at becoming more well-rounded." They all laughed.

Mr. John continued, "You too will have your own strengths, and someday maybe you will be called upon to share them with other trainees like yourself. It is always best to learn from someone who is not only good at something, but who can also demonstrate it and teach it as well. If you wanted to be a great golfer, you would get a coach like Hank Haney, and if your focus was putting or short game, you'd call Dave Pelz. Do you understand?"

Thomas replied clearly, "Yes, sir."

"So, do you know what courtesy is?" Mr. John began.

Thomas looked puzzled. "I think I know what being courteous is—or I guess I know how to be courteous. But I'm not sure I can tell you the exact definition of courtesy."

Mr. John laughed. "You can exchange the word for politeness if it helps. Can you define *politeness*?"

Thomas struggled again and gave a nervous laugh. "Can I Google it?"

Victor replied, "I don't think you are going to need to. That is why we are here. Mr. John knows more about this subject than just about anyone on the planet."

Mr. John bowed humbly. "I'm not sure about that, but thank you for the kind words." He turned to Thomas and said, "Let me help you. Many people find both words difficult to define. But Webster defines courtesy as 'the showing of politeness in one's attitude and behavior toward others.' So that is why I said the words were interchangeable. Have you ever heard someone say, 'You are too courteous'?"

"No, I can't say that I have," Thomas replied.

Mr. John continued, "I've heard people say, 'He was a very polite young man,' or say that someone was courteous. But it's funny how you never hear people say that a person was *too* polite or courteous. They use the word *polite*, because that's the action or behavior of someone being courteous." Thomas nodded but didn't interrupt. "So, a long time ago, I decided, because of the belief system that was instilled in me as a child and that I confirmed as an adult, that a person can never be too polite."

Now Thomas looked confused.

Mr. John elaborated. "Some examples of courtesy would be covering your mouth when you sneeze, saying 'Excuse me' when you bump into someone, avoiding swearing, not interrupting people when they are speaking, monitoring your electronics when in public, offering assistance when you see someone in need—are you getting the idea?"

Thomas smiled, nodded, and said, "Definitely."

Victor added, "Mr. John could go on all day."

Mr. John said, "I don't think you can be too polite or courteous, and it's hard to be either without being nice. You just don't see many mean polite people."

Thomas said, "Well, not to be argumentative, but soldiers who show military courtesy aren't always nice."

Mr. John said, "Good point. I had never thought of that, though soldiers certainly learn courtesy and practice it. Standing at attention, removing their hat indoors, saluting—these are all forms of military courtesy. But soldiers can come across as mean, can't they—good point!" Thomas sat up proudly.

Mr. John leaned forward and whispered, "There's one thing that I think you will find to be true as you go through your training. Your mentors will always work to teach you, that's what they love to do, but I can bet you'll probably get just a little more out of them if you are extremely courteous and polite. Don't you tend to want to help and go out of your way for people who are polite and courteous to you?"

"Yes. I bend over backward for people who are really polite, courteous, or nice."

Mr. John asked, "Are you in need of anything yet? A drink perhaps?"

The two men shook their heads and Victor replied, "I think we are okay for now."

Mr. John resumed his lesson. "When it comes to courtesy, you also need to be aware of cultural differences. For instance, in many countries it is customary for the man to walk in front of a women, to eat first, or to be seated on a bus or train while the woman stands."

Thomas raised his eyebrows. "Wow, my mother would have smacked me if I didn't stand and let a woman have a seat on the train."

"So, in business, it is important to know and understand the people you are dealing with, as they may think something is perfectly normal that you would never accept, or vice versa."

Mr. John continued, "There are some things we will want you to do no matter what. These courtesies shouldn't offend anyone. For instance, as you are introduced to each of the companies that Brad is associated with, you will notice that employees always stand and greet a customer when they enter the establishment. If the employee is on the phone or working behind a monitor, they will still look up, smile, make eye contact, and acknowledge the person's presence with a head nod or wave of the hand. Once the call is over, they will stand, apologize for any delay, and offer assistance—no matter how often that customer comes in."

"That's impressive," Thomas said.

Victor spoke for a moment. "We set our standards as high as possible, and they are to be applied anywhere, but of course without causing controversy or offending anyone. We would never intentionally do that."

Mr. John nodded. "Victor says 'applied anywhere.' Think about the different regions of the United States for a second. If you were walking down the street in New York City, you probably couldn't get anyone to make eye contact with you, let alone give you a smile and greeting. Yet, if you were in Kingfisher, Oklahoma, and someone said 'good morning,' that might turn into a fifteen-minute conversation. It's just a different expectation and pace of life. If you board a subway in the city, you'll probably have to bump into lots of people, or miss getting on. If you bump into someone in a small town, where there is a great deal of open space, you had better say 'excuse me' or you may get a stern talking to. Part of the problem is the hustle and bustle of big cities, but I think there are other contributing factors." Mr. John pointed to the computer on his desk.

He continued, "How about the fact that we are living in the Internet age?"

Victor grinned and chimed in, "Yeah, how about it?"

Thomas and Mr. John laughed and Mr. John continued, "Thanks to technology, you can send thousands of messages a day and never have face-to-face interaction, never speak to that person, and actually don't even know whether they are even a real person."

Victor added, "Even though it's not as personal, I make it a point to respond to every text and email—unless the person is just saying 'You're welcome' because I said 'Thank you' to them. I also attach a photo of myself, so they know whom they are communicating with. If someone sends me a thank-you, I always say 'You're welcome.' If I get a text, email, or correspondence, I reply to let them know I received it and give a brief update about what will happen next. It's common courtesy and helps ensure great communication."

Mr. John resumed, "I can't tell you how many times a day I have to follow up with someone to ensure they received an email, because they don't respond. It's unproductive for me, so I have to believe it is happening to others and disrupting their workday as well. We can't assume everything will work out perfectly when we hit Send. I've had people send important, time-sensitive documents that ended up in my spam folder. In many cases, I didn't find them until it was too late. Then, when I spoke to the person who sent the message, their response went something like, "Well—I sent it—I did my part. That's your responsibility." They treated it like a hot potato; once it left their hands, they were done. I would say that isn't very courteous."

He continued, "The same goes for phone etiquette. It starts with how you answer the phone. A proper greeting with a welcoming tone is important. People also complain about someone calling and not leaving a message, or leaving multiple similar messages. One way to become more efficient and productive is to always answer your phone. It lets people know you value their call. If you shouldn't be talking on your phone because you are in a meeting, an office, or on a plane, then turn it off. But immediately after you notice missed calls or messages, call them back."

Mr. John sat back in his chair and sighed. "We could talk about courtesy all day long, and then inevitably we have to be polite and courteous." He reached behind his desk and pulled a book from his credenza. He picked up a pen and began to write inside the front cover. Then he handed the book to Thomas, who cradled it carefully and read the title, "Creating a Common Courtesy Culture."

"Thank you very much, Mr. John. I will read every word."

Victor added, "Not just read, but practice everything that's in the book as well, right?"

"Right," Thomas agreed.

Mr. John added, "I'm sure you have realized by now that each mentor could easily spend more than one day teaching their subject. The goal is to give you an introduction to the topic, possibly provide material to study on your own, and then to be a resource you can call upon whenever you need further assistance."

Victor put in, "It's like having a team of superheroes at your disposal." Thomas laughed.

Victor glanced at his watch and stood, giving Thomas a hint it was time to leave. He said, "Mr. John, it was a pleasure. I am sure it will have been a valuable investment of your time."

Thomas agreed. "I know for me it was priceless."

Mr. John laughed deeply. "Your kind words will get you everywhere." He walked the two out to the front of the store and waved as they got in the car to leave.

As they drove, Thomas was conscious of trying to be as courteous as possible to both Victor and the driver. Once he arrived home, he stayed outside for a little while and practiced on the postman, his neighbors, and some kids who were playing in the street. He went into the house, ate dinner, and spent the rest of the night writing down everything he remembered from the day in his journal. When he began to get sleepy, he made his way into his bedroom. As he was settling in, he accidently knocked the television remote off the nightstand. Just then he realized he hadn't turned his television on in almost a week. He smiled to himself, lay down, and fell fast asleep.

CHAPTER 7

===

My failures have been errors in judgment, not of intent.
—Ulysses S. Grant

Please Don't Judge a Book by Its Cover

Thomas rolled over, rubbed the sleep out of his eyes, and noticed it was overcast and gray outside the window. He lay there, unmotivated, second-guessing the last few days. As his eyes slowly scanned his room, he saw the ring box on his dresser. The pain of his past mistakes shot through him, and he realized that if he continued to lie there with negative thoughts swirling around in his head, he'd never turn his life around. He leaped out of bed, ate breakfast, and got ready just before the car arrived. He made that morning's trip in silence.

The car pulled up in front of an old red brick building with a blue painted sign that read, LANCASTER'S MEDICAL SUPPLY. Thomas exited the car and the driver said, "I'll pull around and wait in the parking lot behind the building."

Thomas walked to the entrance, pushed the glass door open and noticed several elderly people moving about. His attention was drawn to a well-dressed man in a wheelchair accompanied by a tall woman. Together they were examining walking canes. Although he was missing both legs and one arm, the man was using his one hand to sort through the display. Thomas walked to the counter and asked for Mr. Lancaster, just as he was told to. The young woman behind the counter hung up the phone, stood, smiled, and said politely, "He'll be with you in just a bit. I've been asked to show you to his office to wait. Would you mind following me?"

"Not at all, lead the way," Thomas replied. They quickly arrived in an office.

"Please make yourself comfortable."

"Thank you very much."

Thomas stood still for a minute wondering what life must be like for the couple up front, who are dealing not only with old age, but also his disability. He looked around the office. There were shelves chock full of plaques, awards, and autographed memorabilia all with the name Harold Lancaster on them. Above the desk hung a 101st airborne banner with a photo of a young soldier in full military dress. Filling up loads of space around the office were pictures of what seemed to be a beautiful wife and two lovely children. This space seemed to be the shrine of a man who apparently had the perfect life. On the bookshelves Thomas saw shelf after shelf of books on leadership and personal and professional development.

Suddenly, the door opened and, to Thomas's surprise, the man in the wheelchair rolled into the office. "Thomas I presume?"

Thomas stood stunned.

"You are Thomas, aren't you?"

Thomas nodded and replied, "Yes, sir," shaking hands with the man.

"My name is Mr. Lancaster, but you can call me Harold. I apologize for your wait."

Thomas was still a bit shocked. This man was not a customer at all but rather the owner and one of the mentors. Remembering his lesson about courtesy, he smiled and said, "Thank you so much for taking the time to meet with me. I am looking forward to learning whatever you are willing to teach."

Harold raised his arm and waved it around the room, "So, be honest—because I know that was the first lesson you learned—were you expecting someone else?"

"Yes, I was. Honestly, when I came into the store I thought you were a customer."

Harold chuckled. "That's very curious, considering the topic I am going to share with you today." Thomas looked interested and Harold continued, "But we'll get to that in a few minutes. Let me ask, do you think with what you have learned so far, and seen in here, you could paint an accurate picture of who I am? I mean, you got to spend a few minutes in here. I'm sure you looked around."

"Well, there's a lot to take in—but I'm pretty observant and I've got a lot to work from." Thomas looked around the room one more time and nodded confidently. "I think so."

Harold whispered conspiratorially, "Would you like to guess what the topic is, before you share your thoughts about who I am?"

Thomas looked less confident suddenly and shook his head no. "I was already wrong about you being a customer. I better just wait for you to tell me."

Harold smiled, "It's so appropriate now. If I could have caught you before you came in the store, I would have said, Please don't judge a book by its cover."

Thomas grinned widely. "That's hilarious. Because that's exactly what I was doing, isn't it?"

"People do it every day. But we're going to train that out of you, aren't we?"

"No doubt, I'm all ears and raring to go."

"How about let's go for a walk?" Harold began to maneuver the wheelchair toward the front door. He said loudly to the girl at the counter, "We are going out for a bit. Call me on my cell if you need something."

In a moment, Thomas and Harold were down the sidewalk and around the building. They stopped at a little gathering area, with some shade trees, chairs, and a small table that Harold could pull his wheelchair up to. During the short walk, Thomas thought, *Having Harold in a medical supply house was genius. He's the perfect person to understand the need for beds, canes, wheelchairs, any medical supplies, since he is physically challenged and actually uses the products he sells. He seems to be someone who can to talk to customers, empathize with them, and be able to uncover and comprehend their needs.*

Harold motioned to a chair. "Please take a seat, young man."

Thomas sat down, "Thank you again for meeting with me—it looks as though you are a very busy man."

Harold grinned. "I keep busy, but never too busy for a new recruit. Brad and Victor tell me you have promise—that you are catching on very quickly."

"That's kind of them to say. I am working hard at it."

Harold continued, "If you'll indulge me, I'd like to share a few things with you this afternoon. No need for note taking, nor are there exercises for you to perform—just sit back and listen to a guy in a wheelchair. I know you're a visual learner, and I think I'll paint a pretty clear picture with my story. When I'm through, I hope you'll have received the value that is hidden within the words that I'll share."

He motioned to his legs and arm. "First, you should know I wasn't born this way. Nope—unfortunately this was the result of heavy drinking, drugs, and a bad decision. It was a Saturday evening and, as was my custom, I had been sneaking Jack and Coke most of the day and working on my Harley in the garage. My wife and two kids had been in the house watching television and playing games. She always took care of the children and allowed me to have my own space that one day of the week." He looked a bit emotional.

Thomas asked, "Would you like me to get you a drink or something?"

Harold swallowed hard. "No, thank you. Just bear with me a second, please."

Regaining his composure, he continued, "Just like clockwork, around five that evening, I heard the rumble of my next door neighbor driving up. We exchanged greetings and slid over by my workbench. I pulled out a vial that I kept and laid down two lines of cocaine for us to snort." Thomas's eyes grew big. He looked extremely surprised. Harold continued, "Just about the time we finished wiping the powder from our noses, my wife walked in. She came out to remind me that she was planning to take the children out for dinner that night." Harold stopped and pointed at Thomas, "And, before you ask, my wife had no idea that my neighbor or I had ever taken drugs. She was totally against them, and didn't like my drinking either—she was a good woman." Thomas sat in disbelief.

Harold continued, "Well, that's when the *you-know-what* hit the fan. I was trying to step in front of my neighbor, to keep my wife from seeing the vial in his hand. But, as I did, I bumped him and he dropped it on the garage floor. My wife saw it immediately and said, 'Is that what I think it is?' My neighbor didn't speak, but he had guilt written all over his face. He bent and picked up the vial. My wife turned to me and said, 'Are you doing drugs?' Before I could reply, my neighbor spoke and said, 'No, they're mine. Your husband didn't know I brought them, and I'm sure if he did, he would have made me leave.'" Harold shrugged. "So, I went along with it and acted like I was crazy mad. I pushed him out of the garage and cursed at him. He quickly made a beeline for his house. I hugged my wife and apologized."

"Wow, and she bought it?"

Harold nodded. "She loved me, and she didn't want to believe I'd do something so stupid. So, after things calmed down, we changed the plan, grabbed the kids, and headed out to dinner together. And yes, I was as high as a kite. We were only a few miles from the house when I remember my wife saying, 'Honey, you need to slow down.' And that's when everything changed." Harold now began to sob uncontrollably. Thomas was at a loss, but quickly got his handkerchief out of his pocket and presented it to the man. Harold just sat there for a few minutes, and Thomas didn't know what to do. He had no idea how to console the man.

After several moments Harold began to regain his composure. "Well, it was the last thing I remember from that day. The next thing I know, I'm waking up in a hospital bed trying to figure out where my arm and legs went. As I tried to move, out of the corner of my eye I noticed my neighbor, who was asleep in a chair in my hospital room. Then I heard someone ask, "Do you know where you are?" It was the nurse.

My neighbor woke up, but he stayed out of the way while the nurse tended to me. I remember her asking if I knew my name. For some reason I could hear her, but I couldn't respond. She informed me that I had been in a medically induced coma for three weeks and I found out later that my neighbor had been there by my side almost the entire time." Harold wiped the remaining tears from his cheek with Thomas's handkerchief and held it up. "Thank you for this."

"You are more than welcome. Anything else I can do?"

Harold shook his head no. "Well, that was thirteen years ago. And not a minute goes by that I don't miss them." Thomas's eyes grew huge. "Yes, I lost an arm, two legs, my wife, and both children. After I got healthy enough, I still had to stand trial and spent ten years behind bars. I felt in my own heart and still do that I deserved the death penalty." Thomas was blown away, trying to comprehend this tragic story. Harold continued, "Many lives were changed that day, and one of them was someone you know." Thomas looked puzzled. "My neighbor, the man at my bedside—well, you know him as Brad."

Thomas thought for a minute and began to sort it all out. Brad had said his life had changed thirteen years ago, and now, hearing the story, he could see how. He could easily understand how the topic of honesty mattered so much in everything you do. "So, why would you still be friends with Brad after all that?"

The sun was now shining in Harold's eyes, but he was so focused it didn't seem to bother him. He went on, "Brad has always felt responsible for the accident. That's the day he decided never to lie again, gave up drugs, and made a number of other changes in his life. He still thinks if he had told my wife the truth, she might have left me, but she and the kids would be alive today and I'd have my arm and legs back. He's spent every day since then trying to make it up to me. He stayed by my side during my rehab and worked to pay off all my medical bills. He visited and wrote to me in prison, as well as paid for my lawyer and helped me get an early release. And now he's my business partner, and that has allowed me to serve others, even with my disability." Thomas thought, *That all makes sense, but what does that have to do with*—" Harold said, "But what does all this have to do with judging a book by its cover, right?" Thomas couldn't believe he had read his mind.

"Did you judge me when you walked in the store and saw me in this wheelchair?" Harold asked. Without letting Thomas answer, he said, "Did you imagine how I ended up in that chair, or what my limitations are, or even what kind of man I might be?" He stared intently at Thomas.

"First I thought you were a customer searching for a cane," Thomas replied. "That made me think about how your life must be. I guess my mind wandered all over the place—"

"Now that you heard my story and have seen my office, did any of it match?" Harold interrupted.

"No, not a bit," Thomas answered easily.

Harold continued, "So, you probably didn't see me as a drunk, druggie, or murderer either? And if you were to look at someone else you could identify as a drunk, druggie, or murderer, you may not be able to see all the good they had done in their life. People are always evolving, changing, and we all have a unique story to tell. That's why we don't judge a book by its cover."

The two men sat silently for a moment.

Harold spoke up. "I'd like you to look at the tip of your finger. See your fingerprint? Believe it or not, you won't find a match for it. Not in the entire history of man. It's one of a kind. Every person's story is one of a kind. You might find some similarities to someone else's story, but they will never be exactly alike. And what a person looks like or acts like today may be one hundred and eighty degrees different from where they were in the past, or where they'll be in the future, for that matter." Thomas nodded in agreement. Harold looked deeply into his eyes. "The trick in life is to read each and every chapter, not just look at the cover or skim through the introduction. If you only judge people by the title of their book, or by the cover, you will miss out on some really great stuff. Sure, you may get fooled once in a while, but if Brad or I had judged each other by our covers, neither one of us would have been given a second chance."

Harold began to push his wheelchair backward. "How about we head back to my office and continue this conversation?"

"Sure, I'm following your lead," Thomas said, standing. The two men made their way back to the front door and into the store. The young woman stood and greeted them with a smile as they continued to the office area.

Harold stopped in the hallway just outside his door and looked at Thomas. "Knowing what you know now, will you look at my office differently?" He opened the door and they entered.

Thomas replied, "Candidly, I'm drawn to the pictures of the beautiful woman and the children—is that your family?"

"Yes, that's them."

"And I am impressed by all the accolades and awards you have received."

"I'd trade them all to go back and make a different decision, as would Brad."

The two remained quiet for a few moments.

Thomas broke the silence. "That was a powerful lesson. I'm wondering how many times I assumed something about a person but was completely wrong? For instance, the girl at your counter: she has piercings and a tattoo. I instantly judged her, but now I realize how unfair that is."

Harold nodded. "Funny that you mention her. I understand that you were just sizing her up based on your past experiences, perhaps. But I can guarantee that you underestimated her. She's an Ivy League grad, speaks French, and has a heart of pure gold. But unfortunately, most people will never take the time to find that out about her." Thomas looked amazed and ashamed.

Harold added, "Now, don't be too hard on yourself. We all can't be like my friend Sammy, who works in law enforcement as an interrogator. He and I frequently get into discussions—or disagreements—about profiling and stereotypes, but he always has me looking at things differently. It's his job to scan for certain types of folks, which actually helps him look at every characteristic a person has. He really pays attention and doesn't get fooled by the things we see. I also understand that as humans, we are always trying to make sense of things, to organize and categorize them, so we can try to control the situation by grouping people. We don't like the unknown, and that goes for people as well."

"Then what are we supposed to do?"

Harold took a moment and then said, "You should follow one of the golden rules of providing great service. When it comes to business and your customer, remember the old adage, *People don't care how much you know until they know how much you care*. It's that simple. Take the time to show them you care. The easiest way to do that is get to know the real them."

Thomas nodded in agreement. Harold's alarm rang and he reached to turn it off. "Well, my good man, I have enjoyed our time together and I truly hope you received value today."

Thomas stood and reached to shake hands. "Yes, sir, I've learned a great deal. I will surely do my best to apply the lesson you taught."

Both men smiled, shook hands, and Thomas left the office. As he walked through the showroom and past the girl at the counter, he said, "au revoir" to her. She beamed and replied, "au revoir." Thomas made his way out to the car, climbed in, and settled in to think about this new lesson on his way home.

CHAPTER 8

*It is our attitude at the beginning of a difficult task which,
more than anything else, will affect its successful outcome.*
—William James

Your Attitude Is Everything

There were lines on Thomas's face when he awoke. He had dreamed about being in a wheelchair, and as he looked down at his intact legs he felt an overwhelming sense of gratitude for the life he had. He rose, got ready, and was reviewing notes when he heard the car pull up in the driveway. Thomas grabbed his stuff and flew out of the house. The car had barely come to a stop when he opened the door and climbed in. "Where are we off to today?"

"Oh, now—you don't want me to ruin the surprise, do you?" the driver replied. The two men exchanged a smile and drove away.

The car stopped at a gated entrance to a large metal industrial building. Always excited to see where he would end up, Thomas saw a sign that read, Go Green Recycling Center. The driver waited for traffic to clear, and then checked in at the guard shack before entering the facility. Several trucks full of trash streamed into the yard and empty ones rolled out. The operation was impossible to see from the road, because the facility had a tall fence around it. They stopped and Thomas got out of the car. Immediately, he was hit by a horrible stench that took his breath away.

The driver told him to go inside and ask for a man by the name of Mark Stanton. As Thomas entered, he was immediately greeted by a worker. "Mr. Thomas, my name is Jillian. I was told you are supposed to meet with Mr. Stanton, but he will be delayed a few minutes because he's fixing a machine. If you'll follow me, I'll get you signed in as a visitor and give you some protective gear, which will also keep you from ruining those nice clothes." Thomas began to think he might be in for a day that wasn't going to be very sensational. He quickly caught himself and realized he needed to stop the *stinking thinking.*

He followed Jillian to a room where he was given a hairnet, helmet, gloves, apron, and plastic boots. Jillian pointed. "That's the men's room, and there should be an open locker to put your belongings in." Thomas changed and returned to meet Jillian, who had him sign in. They walked out into the plant. It was noisy, there were piles of trash everywhere, water was splashing, and the place stank to high heaven. Across the room Thomas could see several men working on one of the conveyors. The belt started moving trash and the men celebrated with high fives.

A man approached with quick, purposeful steps, took off his gloves, and smiled widely. "Hello, I am guessing you are Thomas?"

"That's me."

The man turned to Jillian. "Thanks for getting him set up. I'll take it from here."

Turning to Thomas, he said, "I'm Mark Stanton, your host today." He looked around the facility. "By the look on your face, you probably didn't expect this?"

Thomas smiled. "Not in a million years."

"Well, I think you'll find today's lesson is important. But don't worry—we won't be here long. I just have a few more things to accomplish, and we'll head out. Would you mind lending me a hand?"

"Whatever you need!" Thomas replied eagerly.

"A good attitude—just what I was hoping for."

Thomas stood feeling helpless as he held some tools and Mark adjusted a few conveyors and explained the details of the operation. They made their way back to the locker room to change. Thomas was a little confused. "So, we aren't going to work here all day?

Mark chuckled. "You can stay here and work if you want. You'd definitely witness today's lesson in action here at the plant as well, but my plan takes us somewhere else. I hope that's okay. I'm actually supposed to be off on weekends, but I wanted you to stay on track with your training."

"Thank you. It was very kind of you to meet me on a Saturday. I'm on your schedule today; even though I've learned a great deal already, I'm ready for more." He paused. "Although I haven't heard what the lesson is yet—have I?"

Mark snickered. "No, I didn't reveal the topic yet. But don't worry—you have already shown signs that lead me to believe you won't have a problem with it." Thomas was curious what Mark meant by this.

They gathered their belongings and left the facility in Mark's pickup truck. Mark turned up the radio and they just drove, listening to the music without speaking a word. Thomas thought it was kind of odd, but he had learned not to judge. Mark was giving every indication he was a man who was very happy with his life. He smiled constantly, he was a courteous driver, and he seemed to be in great spirits.

Finally Mark spoke. "Do you like football—I mean soccer?"

"Don't know too much about it, to be honest," Thomas replied.

"Well, they call it football in most other countries around the world. My daughter plays on a team—she's in a camp right now. That's where we're headed."

Thomas smiled. "Well, then, I guess I'm going to learn more about soccer, or football."

Mark pulled into the parking lot of the River Soccer Complex. There were dozens of fields and children kicking balls as far as the eye could see. He parked the truck and the two men got out. It was clear Mark knew exactly where he was going. He made a beeline toward a field that had approximately thirty children and two coaches. Thomas worked hard to keep up. There were bleachers along the side. They took a seat at the end, away from the other parents and onlookers.

Mark said, "We'll sit down here, so we can talk." Thomas was thinking, *Pay attention, because you never know what the lesson is going to be.* He had learned that much in his time in the program.

The children seemed to be having a fantastic time. You could tell the coaches loved what they were doing. Mark's daughter glanced over and saw him. She blew her dad a kiss and went back to her drills.

"Do you know what makes someone really good at what they do?" Mark asked.

Thomas thought for a second. "Well, it could be their specific knowledge of a skill, or whether they really enjoy what they do, or—"

"What about how they go about it?"

"Do you mean their attitude?"

Mark jumped. "We have a winner: their attitude." The two men exchanged a quick knuckle bump.

Mark continued, "Did you notice at the plant today, everyone seemed to have a great attitude? They were all very positive."

"As you are," Thomas observed.

"Thanks. A positive attitude makes all the difference. It can get you over the hump, inspire others to do better, and provide hope when it's needed most." Thomas nodded in agreement. Mark pointed to one of the coaches in the middle of the field. "You see that man right there?"

"The one in blue?"

"Yep. Everyone calls him Timo. He's the guy who taught me the greatest lesson about having a positive attitude. I'll introduce you to him after the session." Thomas focused his attention on the coach. Mark continued, "Since we have about thirty-five minutes before it's over, I'd like to tell you the story I heard Timo's college coach share at an awards banquet in honor of Timo."

"I'd love to hear it."

"Apparently Timo was an incredible soccer player in Kenya, his home country. He played for some of the best teams and actually made it all the way up to his country's national team, which was working hard to qualify for the Africa Cup of Nations. At some point, he applied to come to the United States to attend university and play soccer. He was accepted and offered a scholarship at St. Gregory's, a small Catholic university in Shawnee, Oklahoma. The plane he arrived on landed at eleven o'clock at night, and by the time he got to bed it was early in the morning. Just a few hours after landing, the team was scheduled for physicals with the doctor and then fitness testing in the afternoon. But due to a scheduling error, the team had to reverse the order of the plan.

"So, after a twenty-hour plane ride and not much sleep, Timo turned up that morning and promptly showed he was the class of the field and fitter than anyone. Later that day they boarded buses for the medical center to take physicals. After all the players had been examined, the doctor came out and spoke to the coach. He said, 'Coach, I've found something abnormal with your new Kenyan player's heart, and I'd like to send him across the street for further tests with a cardiologist. Now, it could be that he just flew halfway around the world and hasn't had much sleep. He also told me he participated in training with the team this morning and then promptly ate a big, greasy American lunch. So there may be nothing to worry about, but I want to make sure.' Timo and the coach went across the street to see the specialist.

"After a few tests and a long wait, the cardiologist, Dr. Hope, came out and met with the coach. He asked if the coach had ever heard of Epstein's abnormality. The coach hadn't heard of it. It meant that Timo had a very large hole in his heart. Unfortunately, it would be too risky to operate; the recommendation was to send him back to Kenya. The doctors couldn't predict how long he would live.

"At this point the coach was lost. In a matter of just a few hours, Timo went from being one of the best players to come out of Africa to never being able to play soccer again without risking death. The toughest part was yet to come, because Timo had no idea about his fate. The doctor didn't want to give him the prognosis, especially with no family around and Timo's having just arrived in the U.S. So his coach sat him down to break the news. Bear in mind, Timo had come to the U.S. on an athletic scholarship, so if he couldn't play, he wouldn't be able to stay in school.

"The coach explained everything in detail, breaking down out of sadness several times during the conversation. Never once did Timo cry. After hearing everything the coach had to say, he flashed a smile and said, 'So, I'm not supposed to play soccer again. Is there any way I can keep my scholarship and stay on in another capacity, perhaps as a manager or assistant coach? I think I can help this team win championships, and I can recruit other great players who will want to come to this program.' The coach couldn't believe it. Here he was, telling this man that not only would he never be able to play soccer again, but he could die if he overexerted himself—and Timo never even shed a tear.

"When the coach asked him if he understood the situation, Timo responded by saying, 'Yes, I understand that when one door closes, another one opens. Some people are going to say this is tragic. But I might have never seen a specialist and got this kind of diagnosis in Kenya. My condition might have been overlooked and I could have died. There is no way I was going to be able to play forever, but I can surely offer what I have learned and coach for the rest of my life.' In the coach's mind, there was no decision to be made. Timo became his assistant coach that day and they never looked back.

"Timo went on to graduate and helped St. Gregory's become one of the top-ranked teams in the country, winning championships. He took an assistant's position at another university, earned his masters degree, and went on to coach and win youth and college championships. He is now a head college coach and is regarded as one of the best in the country. Timo works with little kids like my daughter, all the way up to some of the older United States National Team players. To top it off, his name has been brought up as a potential candidate to coach the Kenyan National Team.

"When his coach shared the story, he also said that many years later he asked Timo if he ever cried about the situation. Timo's reply was, 'Sure, but I couldn't let it ruin my life. I was alive—I still had a chance to be involved and follow my greatest passion, even if it was as a coach. I also got a great education, which no one can ever take away, and I was surrounded by people who cared about me as a person, not just as a player.'"

Mark looked deep into Thomas's eyes. "Now, if you can't learn the power of a positive attitude from that story, we need to check your heart. Think about the message, and how many times it must have inspired those teams Timo was associated with. It wasn't a secret— all those players at St. Gregory's knew about Timo's condition. Perhaps that's one of the reasons they did so well. It also might have been because of his infectious smile and constant happiness. He just doesn't allow for any negativity around him or his teams. To this day, his coach is a public speaker who shares that story to inspire others and teach them the importance of a positive attitude."

Thomas had been so riveted on Mark he had forgotten that Timo was present on the field and conducting a training session. There were only a few minutes left, but the two men now turned their attention to the field. The first thing Thomas noticed was that Timo seemed to be having a blast. He thoroughly enjoyed what he was doing. Even when he was correcting the players, he did it with a smile and was very supportive. The players all responded well to him.

At the end, Timo called all the players into the middle of the field and they finished the session with a cheer. Mark's daughter came running, leaped into her dad's arms, and gave him a hug and a big kiss. "How are you today, daddy?"

Mark said, "Thomas, this is my daughter Megan. Can you say hello?"

The girl said shyly, "Hello, Mr. Thomas."

"Hello, Ms. Megan," Thomas replied. "It's very nice to meet you."

After saying goodbye to all the kids and many of their parents, Timo made his way over to the three of them. Thomas stared in awe and then reached out his hand to shake. "Thomas Frickle. It's an honor to meet you."

Timo grinned and replied with an African accent, "Timothy Kibune, but everyone calls me Timo. Pleased to meet you as well." He turned to Mark and gave him a hug. "How are you, my brother?"

"Fantastic—Megan is excited to be attending your camp."

"She is doing very well—she'll be better than I ever was as a player." Megan smiled at the compliment as Mark continued, "Well, it's a beautiful day. I'm off and spending time with my daughter, and I've been able to share your story with this young man who's in our training program."

Timo looked a bit embarrassed. "So, he's been boring you with some old story?

"Boring, no way." Thomas replied. "It is one of the most inspirational stories I've ever heard."

Mark said, interrupting, "See, it never gets old. Now, is anyone hungry?" The others nodded. "How about we grab some lunch?" There was a café close by in the park, which would allow them to eat and enjoy the outdoors.

Megan guessed what her father's plan was. "Are we going to the café? Can I sit by the pond while we eat?"

Mark laughed. "Yes, and of course you can sit by the pond. The grown-ups have a few things to talk about, so you can feed the ducks while you eat."

Mark bought lunch and the three men sat at the table closest to the pond. Megan hurried down to the ducks with her lunch in her hand.

"Timo," Mark began, "as I mentioned to you on the phone last night, I simply wanted to introduce Thomas to you today. I don't expect you to do anything special. I just thought it was important, since he's in the Sensational Group program."

Timo raised his eyebrows and smiled at Thomas. "Quite an undertaking isn't it?"

Thomas replied, "It has been remarkable. In fact, it's changed my life."

"Timo, would you have any words of advice?" asked Mark.

Timo grinned. "Well, I've got a few minutes before I need to start the next session."

"Whatever you are willing to share, I'm all ears," Thomas said.

Timo began, "With soccer, I can demonstrate individual skills and teach tactics, but when it comes to playing with determination and heart, or having a good attitude, those are attributes that players must generate from within. I believe people can learn how to have a positive attitude by seeing other people get desired results, because they were positive. The opposite is also true. If people see results come from having a negative attitude, that too can become their strategy. So, I work hard to lead by example and surround myself with other people who are positive. I recruit players who may not have all the foot skills, but they have a fantastic attitude. And no matter what, I don't allow people or players with bad attitudes around me or my teams."

"That makes total sense," Thomas said.

Timo continued, "So I must ask—how's your attitude?" Before Thomas could answer, he said, "And how's the attitude of the people in your life? The people you surround yourself with? Do you separate yourself from people who have bad attitudes?"

"Well, it's getting much better now. Since starting the program, I've been surrounded by a lot of awesome people. But I see your point, because it was the exact opposite not that long ago."

Mark grabbed up their trash, took it to the can, and went to get his daughter from the pond.

Timo said, "I read a quote once that said, 'Attitude is a choice.' I truly believe that. It's not what happens to you that determines attitude; it's how you choose to respond. It's all in the mind. My attitude was positive before I found out about my heart and it allowed me to deal with that situation. That's why it's so important for us to work with young people. Reach them when they are still in their formative years and give them the emotional tools to have a happy and healthy life."

He continued, "It has been said that if you want to change your surroundings, change the way you look at them. We lift ourselves by our thoughts. If you want to enlarge your life, you must first enlarge how you think about it and about yourself. Hold the ideal of yourself as you long to be, always and everywhere."

Mark returned with Megan and said, "Well, we better let him get back to the fields."

The two men stood and Thomas offered his hand. "Thank you for spending time with us. It was a pleasure meeting you."

"I'm sorry if I wasn't more help. I'm better at teaching soccer than how to have a positive attitude."

"The way you have lived your life will easily teach anyone who wants to learn. They only need to pay attention," Mark assured him.

Timo walked back to the field and Megan got into the truck with Mark and Thomas, to return to the recycling plant so Thomas could meet his ride. Tired from the workout, Megan leaned against her father and took a nap.

Mark said, "I think you will find that people who are happy with their lives, who are chasing their dreams, living every minute to the fullest, and are successful by most definitions are those who have great attitudes. They are not afraid to test themselves and continue stretching their own abilities to experience more in their life."

A driver sped around them, cut them off, and flipped them the bird.

"There is the perfect example. I think we would both agree that person has a bad attitude. And, if I adopt a bad attitude because

90

of what they just did, it could turn into something off-the-charts horrible. If I were to respond, speed up, chase them down, or anything like that, we could quickly find ourselves in a serious road rage situation.

"The entrepreneur and author Jim Rohn wrote, 'Philosophy drives attitude, attitude drives actions, actions drive results, results drive lifestyles.' So, it only makes sense that if you don't like your lifestyle, look at your results. And if you don't like your results, look at your actions, and so on. I know you have worked on your honesty and your beliefs, so I'm guessing you are beginning to have a handle on what your philosophy is?"

Thomas looked lost. "My philosophy?"

"Yes, your philosophy on life, on people, on happiness. Your philosophies will all stem from what you believe, and that's what will drive your attitude."

Thomas sat in deep thought.

Mark continued, "Unfortunate events are going to happen—to you, to those around you, and to people you know. Many people will want to share their negativity with you. Don't buy into their philosophy. Find the silver lining, if you believe there is one to be found. Don't dwell on the bad thing that happened, just deal with how and why to keep your attitude great. Once you start doing it, people around you will begin noticing that you don't lose it when things go wrong. They will call you 'the optimist' and will look to you for support and answers. The negative nellies will realize you aren't going to join in on their whining or pity party, so they will begin to look for solutions and develop a positive attitude, or they will take their negativity to other people who will want to be in their club and aren't trying to better the situation." Thomas nodded in agreement.

Mark went on, "When something negative happens, or someone acts negatively to you, take a minute to remind yourself that something simply happened *to you*. Then decide how you are going to respond to it. There will be people who want to blow your candle out to make theirs look brighter. When something goes wrong, teach them to let their light shine together with others. Don't just have a knee jerk reaction to whatever happens. Attack the situation with a positive attitude. For the rest of your life you'll have challenges, obstacles, and events that don't go your way—everyone will. But be a glass-half-full guy—be like Timo."

"He sets a high standard, but I'll work hard to reach it."

"You've already been introduced to the communication component of this training," Mark continued, "so you understand the importance of choosing your words carefully and in ways that accentuate the positives. Start discussions with phrases like, 'This is what I like about—.' Be inclusive in your communication and actions, not exclusive. Highlight all the good, and remind yourself and others when things work out well. People will begin to believe you are blessed and fortunate. They will want to know your secret, because it will seem like everything is working out for you. There is an old adage that says, 'Everything works out for those who outwork others.' So, yes, it will take some work to develop that positive attitude, but the results will be worth it."

"It is kind of difficult," Thomas interjected, "because there is no formula or seven-step program to obtaining a positive attitude."

"There are other ways to see things though. Do you enjoy being around people with negative attitudes?"

Thomas replied, "Not at all."

"That's probably because you already have a positive attitude, for the most part—maybe you just need to go full time. Think about all the effects of having a negative attitude: it drains your energy, blocks positive and creative thoughts, causes stress and worry, and chases away people who are optimistic. One negative person can bring down or ruin an entire team or group if those people aren't strong and positive. That's why you have to protect yourself, friends, loved ones, and just keep away from them."

Mark added sternly, "Some people may think I am telling you to be selfish when I say protect yourself from them. How many positive outcomes have you ever had starting with a negative attitude? You may luck into a few sales, or accounts—but that usually isn't the case. My mother used to say, 'You will become who you hang out with.' So if you hang out with people who have negative attitudes all the time, what do you think will happen to you? If you want to develop a positive attitude, find positive people to be around. It will be much easier to adopt that attitude if you are submerged in it and experience it all the time.

"My positive attitude is in place," Mark continued quietly. "When people tell me I can't do something, I just chuckle. It is my trained, auto response that I have set as a trigger to remind myself not to get upset; instead I think it's funny that other people have no idea what I am capable of. You must 'know thyself.' Being self-aware is based on attention and focus. How you think about yourself, your skills, your abilities, your interaction with others, and your purpose will direct your attitude. The first hurdle is believing at your core that a positive attitude is up to *you*. Your attitude should *never* be a response to what happens to you—it is about how you respond to stimulus. Grasp that, and a positive attitude is right around the corner."

Mark pulled the truck into the parking lot, where Thomas's car was waiting. He said, "Thanks for working around my schedule today."

"If you hadn't told me, I would have thought it was perfectly planned." Thomas replied. "I had a great day and learned a very valuable lesson from you and Timo."

"Well, if you need an attitude adjustment at any point, you know where to find me. Keep up the great work—you are going to be a fantastic addition to the group."

Thomas thanked him, closed the door quietly, and waved goodbye as he headed across the lot.

As Thomas climbed into the car, he found a note that read, "A positive attitude is easy to achieve. Using it to make the world a better place is a more difficult task. Accomplish the first one quickly, so you can begin on the second." Under the note was a plaque that read, *Unlike the weather, your attitude is something you can always control.*

CHAPTER 9

What's Your Purpose in Life?

The sun hadn't come up yet, and Thomas was sitting in his living
room staring through the darkness. The room was quiet and the
thumping in his chest reminded him of Timo's story. In the past,
Thomas would have considered what he was doing as just "killing
time." But now he was keeping his mind engaged, working to
go over every lesson he had learned so far. He continued to test
his beliefs and think about what each of the new mentors had
said to him. Having been in the program a week, each day he
felt more energized than the one before. Even when he stayed
up late, the following morning he would wake before his alarm
went off. His high level of enthusiasm and excitement was a
direct result of learning new things that made him feel more
valuable. Thomas had no idea where it would end up, but he
knew his life was going in the right direction and he had new
hope for a great future.

As the sun began to peek through the window, Thomas
showered and got ready for another fantastic day. After breakfast,

he went outside to greet the beautiful morning. He waved happily at the people across the street as they left for what he thought was probably church, since they were dressed well and it was Sunday. He spoke to a woman who was walking her dog, and took his next-door neighbors their paper. He could feel a positive difference deep in his core, and he was ready to share it with the world. He went back into the house to wait for his transportation, which wouldn't arrive for another hour.

Thomas sat on the couch in deep thought and realized it had been over a week since he had talked to Sandy. He hadn't taken the time to call or let anyone know what was going on. Suddenly, a wave of emptiness overwhelmed Thomas as he realized that no one had tried to contact him either. Initially this made him sad, but he quickly gained control of his emotions and convinced himself it was a temporary situation—his life would soon be better than it had ever been. The sound of the engine as the car pulled into his driveway grabbed his attention. He was eager to find out where he was headed today.

Thomas hopped up and went to the driveway, but before he could reach for the car door, it opened and out stepped a very short, bubbly teenage girl. Thomas immediately noticed she was bald. She had some makeup on, wore trendy clothes, and had a smile that made the sun pale in comparison.

The driver came around and made the introductions. "Mr. Thomas, I'd like to introduce Tonya Stewart. Ms. Tonya, this is Thomas Frickle."

With a slightly curious look, Thomas offered his hand. "Very nice to meet you."

"It's nice to meet you too," Tonya replied. I've heard a lot about you."

"So, I'll be back in two hours then," the driver said. "is that correct, Ms. Tonya?"

She smiled. "Yes, please. I can't be late—my mother would have a cow."

The driver got back into the car and left. Thomas stood frozen for a moment, feeling a little awkward. He was used to leaving, and now there he was alone in his driveway on a Sunday morning with a teenage girl. He said, "I'm sorry if I seem a bit lost, this is a little different than how my other days have gone. I don't want to assume—"

"Don't worry," she interrupted him. "There won't be too much that's normal about our meeting today." She spoke confidently. "I've learned this is how life really works: one minute you have a routine, and the next everything's out of whack." She smiled a big smile and Thomas gave her a halfhearted grin. "I know I'm a lot younger than your other mentors, but don't worry, I think you'll like the lesson I have to share." She motioned toward the house. "So, I guess we'll go back inside?"

"You know, it probably would be more respectful and appropriate if we sat out here. The weather is nice today if you wouldn't mind."

Tonya nodded in agreement. "Yeah, my parents would appreciate you thinking like that. Sitting on the porch will be perfect."

The young girl glanced around Thomas's property in admiration. "Very nice. I heard you live here alone."

Thomas gained his confidence, "For now. My plan kind of got sidetracked."

"So, will you be able to put it back on track?"

"Well, a week ago I wouldn't have thought it was possible, but now I have hope—I believe it will turn out just the way I dreamed!"

"I hope it does. So, you have to be wondering why a bald teenage girl is asking you all these questions about your personal life?"

Thomas giggled. "Of course I am." He motioned to the steps. "Would you like to sit?" Tonya sat on the steps and Thomas joined her. "To be honest, every day of my training has been different. I'm sure there's a good reason you're here today."

Tonya began, "We're going to talk about a subject that you should easily understand in just a few short minutes, but it may take a lot longer to figure out an answer to a question I'll ask you later. First, let

96

me explain why I'm the one sharing this topic." Thomas sat forward and turned toward her attentively as she spoke. "Now, I'd like to think I have great taste, so I can positively tell you I would have never chosen this hairstyle. This one is courtesy of cancer." Thomas felt a heavy heart for her, though Tonya seemed extremely strong. She continued, "I was diagnosed when I was sixteen and have battled like a champ. I've been in remission twice before. Now, I hope this time is it. As you can imagine, it's not what you expect to be doing as a teenager." A look of sorrow was written on Thomas's face, which she must have seen. "Hey, don't feel a bit sorry for me, I'm living a more fulfilled life than most healthy, grown adults that are walking this planet."

Tonya paused for a second, looking directly into Thomas's eyes. "Let's put all the cancer stuff aside for a second and get back to why I'm here. I have one simple but important question for you: What is your purpose?" Thomas froze and then lowered his head as he realized he didn't have a good answer. Tonya let the question sink in a bit longer. "It's a pretty simple question. Many people can easily answer it. For instance, Brad's answer is 'to aid others, act on ideas, and achieve results.' So, what's your purpose?"

Thomas rolled his eyes. "Well, you were right—it may take me a while to come up with a good answer."

She sighed good-naturedly. "It's okay if you don't know right this minute, but it won't be all right if you don't figure it out. I know you've been working on beliefs, communication, attitude, and a number of other lessons—and though you weren't introduced to this lesson first, I believe it's the most important one. Not because it's mine, but it's the one question that most people never get around to answering. Heck, unfortunately, most don't even know to ask it. They go through their entire life and never have a purpose. What's so tragic about that is that if they had found their purpose early, it would have changed not only their whole life, but every person they touched as well."

Thomas took a deep breath. "To me, it kind of sounds like the old question, What do you want to be when you grow up?"

Tonya laughed. "Big difference. I still don't know the answer to that one, but I do know my purpose. You aren't alone; lots of people confuse what they do for a living with their purpose."

She continued, "When they first told me I had cancer, my parents and I were sitting in the doctor's office holding hands. Mom and Dad instantly broke down when the doctor gave us the news. It didn't hit me at first. I only lost it after seeing my father cry. That was my first time. A few days later, the three of us had a long conversation. I found out their initial sadness was because they thought I was being cheated. They felt I wasn't going to experience a full life if I passed away at a young age. After we spoke, I spent some time alone, just thinking. Even though I was young, I had several questions that I needed to answer." She leaned forward and Thomas shifted to meet her. "I asked whether living a full, happy life comes down to how many days you are alive? Does it matter if your parents outlive you? Will people who know me think I had a horrible life if it's cut short? I looked for answers to these questions, plus at least a dozen more. At the end of it all, I came to a realization." Thomas's eyes opened wide in anticipation. "If I knew what my life's purpose was, and could show evidence I was fulfilling it, then it wouldn't matter how long I lived or how I died, it would have been a life well spent."

Thomas was silent a moment, awed by Tonya's maturity. "So, I guess just like Brad, you know what your purpose is?"

Tonya chuckled. "I guess I ought to, or it was the wrong choice for me to come and speak to you. It is actually my father who works with Brad, but he knows our family well and asked me to be involved in the training." She sat back with confidence and contentment, but she never provided an answer, Thomas noticed. He waited, hoping she would share her purpose.

Tonya continued, "Have you ever heard of Mother Theresa?"

"Yes."

"What do think her purpose was?"

Thomas shrugged. He really didn't know.

"Her purpose was really very simple. It was to *ease the suffering of others.* It wouldn't have mattered if she were a doctor, schoolteacher, cook, or any other occupation—her purpose would have been the same. Like earlier, when you mentioned knowing what you wanted to be when you grow up, most people mistakenly define themselves by the type of work they do, not by what their purpose is. I'll bet if someone asked what you do, you'd respond by saying you're a salesman, right?"

"I would."

She jumped on the opportunity. "But is your purpose in life just to sell? I would hope not. Perhaps a better answer is that your purpose is really to fill the needs of others by finding valuable options." Thomas looked suspicious. She added, "To you, that may sound the same, but it's nowhere close. If you want to look back on your life and judge whether it was a success by how much you sold—well, I'd probably feel very sorry for you. But if you want your success to be determined by how many people you helped, honestly, and with an attitude of service—now, that's having a decent purpose for your life. Do you see the difference?"

"Definitely."

Relaxing now, the two continued to talk about other things— her cancer, his past. The time flew as they got to know each other better.

Tonya's wristwatch chimed, and Thomas realized their short time together had come to an end. The car turned onto the street and pulled into the driveway.

Tonya said, "Companies have mission statements. It's what they hang their hat on every day. They also have vision statements to give them direction for the future. Your purpose statement can give you both. If you don't find your own purpose in life, someone else will surely find one for you, and it may not be to your benefit. Remember, only a victim has no answer, and neither of us is a victim—are we?"

"Not at all," Thomas answered quickly.

"Then go be a victor instead. You can do that by finding your purpose, and then living it to the fullest."

"So how do I figure out my purpose?"

"It's not as hard as you might think. Some people make a list of things they love to do. Others figure out what they would do if money weren't an object. I love the exercise where you pretend you're standing at the pearly gates and St. Peter is deciding whether your works on earth will get you into heaven—I don't think he's going to consider what your sales figures were for your career." They both laughed and she added, "There are lots of ways. Think about what you are passionate about, what would make your family proud, what you want written on your tombstone."

Thomas grinned. "I think I get it."

The two stood as the driver got out and opened the rear door. "I'm coming, I'm coming," Tonya called out. She turned and shook hands firmly with Thomas. "I'll check back with you soon. Let me know if there's anything else I can do to help." She grinned widely. "Also, the next time we're together, I'd love to know what you think my purpose is." Thomas remembered that she had never told him. He waved goodbye and thought, *Since she was a young girl with cancer, and seemed very determined, perhaps her purpose was to use her unique situation to inspire others?* In a flash, she was in the car and they were driving away. Thomas paused for a moment and wondered, *What would a sensational purpose be?*

CHAPTER 10

═══════════════════════════════

Time is the most valuable thing a man can spend.

—Theophrastus

1,440 Minutes Make Up a Day

Thomas sat eating breakfast at his kitchen counter. The doorbell surprised him as he took his last bite. He glanced at the time and was confused, because the driver wasn't supposed to pick him up for another hour. He opened the door to find a courier holding a package. Thomas signed the electronic clipboard, closed the door, and went back to the kitchen. He grabbed a knife and carefully opened the box, revealing a beautifully carved clock and an envelope. Thomas eagerly pulled the clock out and opened the envelope. The card read, "I hope this gift warms your new home. Your friend, Brad." Admiring his beautiful gift, Thomas walked into his living room to ponder where he'd put it. He found a perfect spot to hang it so it could be seen when people entered, but he realized he had probably better hang it later that night, since he was leaving soon. He set the clock down carefully and hurried off to shower.

Just as he finished combing his hair, the doorbell startled him for the second time that morning. Thomas smiled to himself in the mirror and then headed out, eagerly anticipating another adventure. As with every day before, the driver greeted him.

Thomas slid into the backseat of the car and the door was shut behind him. Feeling privileged to be exploring exciting places and meeting new people, he promised himself he wasn't going to mess up this opportunity. They drove for about a half hour and came to a stop at a strip mall. Thomas had to laugh when he saw they had parked at a store that serviced and sold clocks. He should have known his trip would have a connection to the gift he had received earlier that morning.

As he stepped out onto the sidewalk, he looked skyward. Rising above the top of the building was a four-sided clock tower that closely resembled Big Ben in London. The sign below the clock read, TIMELESS TREASURES. As he walked closer, the huge clock began to chime loudly. Thomas reached the entrance and had to strain to hear the well-dressed doorman who greeted him. He thought the man said, "Welcome Thomas, we've been expecting you." Then the chimes stopped and the doorman continued, "I hope you enjoy every minute of your time here today. If you wouldn't mind following me, I'll take you to meet Mr. Schilling." The two men walked through the showroom and slipped behind the counter, through a door, and into an office.

There, behind a beautiful wooden desk, sat Mr. Heinz Schilling— the spitting image of Santa Claus. He smiled as he stood to greet Thomas. Speaking with a German accent, he said, "Ah, Thomas, come in, come in." He shook Thomas's hand and motioned for him to sit.

"Will that be all, Mr. Schilling?" the doorman said.

Mr. Schilling looked at Thomas and asked, "Would you like something to drink, or anything else?" Thomas replied, "No, thank you, I'm fine."

"I guess we are good for now, Thanks, Chris." The man exited and closed the door as Thomas glanced around the office.

Mr. Schilling began, "So, I'm told you're making a big shift in your life—is this true?"

Thomas smiled and nodded. "Yes, sir, a huge one."

"Good for you. There's no time like the present. I know very well how busy you have been since beginning the program. I'm sure you've had one full day after another, correct?"

"I've been very busy, even over the weekend."

"Have you been using your time wisely—making the most of every minute?"

"I feel that I have. Most of the time has been scheduled for me, so I go when and where I'm told every day."

"Let me ask," Mr. Schilling continued, "does it seem like you were more productive before you started the training or since?"

Thomas thought for a second. "You know, now that you mention it, I do seem to be getting a lot more accomplished. I seem to be making the most of my time."

Mr. Schilling laughed. "That's wonderful to hear. Do you happen to know how many minutes there are in a day?"

Thomas did the math quickly in his head. "Fourteen hundred and forty?"

"Precisely! Well, I guess there are a few more every once in a while, if you want to be technical. They add those up and that's why we get an extra day every four years. But we all have the same amount of time each day to live our lives, that's what's most important."

He continued, "Now, some people believe that certain moments in life are more important than others. Personally, I believe they all have equal value and are blank slates before we fill them up. Sure, you may remember some moments more than others, moments that seem significant in some way, but each of those fourteen hundred and forty minutes is equal to the others and provides the same opportunity to be used. It bothers me deeply when someone uses a phrase like 'I'm just killing time' or 'I've got all the time in the world.' As Henry David Thoreau wrote, 'As if you could kill time without injuring eternity.' It's unfortunate that they don't understand the true value of that moment, and they never may."

"Unless they are like me and get an opportunity for someone to step into their life and teach them," Thomas replied.

Mr. Schilling smiled. "Ah, you are a quick one, aren't you."

He continued, "As you can see, I love clocks—or any timepiece, for that matter." He indicated the dozens of clocks around his office. "There are a lot of clocks here. The ones in my office are part of my personal collection. I have all kinds, shapes, and sizes. If you take a moment, you will notice some are keeping perfect time, and some have stopped working. Not many people know this, but I stopped those clocks on purpose. They are set to a specific time and remind me of a pivotal moment in my life."

Thomas was curious. "Do you mind if I ask what you mean?"

Mr. Schilling pointed to a clock on the wall that was stopped. "You see that clock? It's stopped at that particular moment because that's when Alexander, a very good friend of mine, passed away last year." Thomas felt sad and was a little bit sorry he asked. "Don't let it upset you. It doesn't bother me. In fact, I use them to pay tribute to people who've been important in my life, as well as to mark specific incidents and key moments.

"Although scientists have theories about it, we haven't found an effective way to warp, save, or stretch time." He winked. "Though it's very possible that Brad has a time machine hidden somewhere." Thomas laughed. "Once ten minutes have ticked off a clock, you never get those minutes back. And don't try to pull the Daylight Savings Time trick, because you have to give that hour back." He added, "It's not like cell phone minutes either; there are no rollovers. You can't save some time today and use it later. Once it's gone, it can never be replaced."

The two men were interrupted when a very large cuckoo clock, prominently displayed on the wall above Mr. Schillings' desk, began to chime. Thomas pointed and asked, "What about that one?"

Mr. Schilling said, "Oh, that one. Well, that one represents me. Besides the fact that it is still running, it's cuckoo." Both men laughed loudly. "It's a great reminder that I am still alive, but that

I too could die any day and so I shouldn't waste time." He paused for a second. "I guess the next question would be, Who determines if you are wasting time, right?"

Thomas jumped in, "Well, I thought differently about time before, but after yesterday I think it's pretty simple. If I'm not helping others, enjoying all that life has to offer, and fulfilling my purpose, I am probably wasting time."

Mr. Schilling looked pleasantly surprised. "That, my new friend, was one of the most profound statements I have ever heard." Thomas was grateful for the compliment and sat up a little straighter.

Mr. Schilling went on, "A smart guy like you already knows this and it sounds silly to even mention, but the clock and the idea of time are human inventions. Yes, there are seasons on our planet and in our lives, but animals don't wear watches—they don't need to know when it's time to sleep, eat, and play. Did you know it is customary to give a watch at a retirement ceremony?" Thomas shook his head no. "Giving a watch at retirement is a symbol that you are now on your own time, instead of the company's time."

"I hadn't really even thought about it before, but that makes total sense."

Mr. Schilling continued, "I won't bore you with trivia any longer. But I hope to give you a few more ideas about how to view time, if that's okay?"

"I'd love to hear more," Thomas said eagerly.

Mr. Schilling paused before continuing. "When you think about time, think about the pyramids. They are enormous structures, but they were built one stone at a time and each block was about the same size. So, think of your life as a pyramid and each minute as one block. When you know what kind of life you want to build, because you have a purpose, you can construct your life by placing minutes together one on top of another. If you have a long life, and stay on purpose, perhaps you will build a huge pyramid. But if, unfortunately, your stay on this earth is cut short, you can still have a beautiful structure, maybe a bit smaller. If you think about it, we are all building some kind of a structure with every minute we spend living."

"So, Mother Theresa would be a good example, right? She knew her purpose and used her time wisely to create a long and fulfilling life. I would say she built her own wonder of the world."

Mr. Schilling beamed. "Correct, and well said. She stacked her moments one on top of another. Remember, most people perform an occupation to earn a living. Here's where this lesson is extremely important. If you can be efficient, and your work also supports your purpose, you can use more of those minutes each day to create a fantastic life. It's also important not to tear down with bad decisions and bad moments what it took you a long time to build with good ones. Managing your time by scheduling your months, days, hours, and minutes allows you to accomplish what is needed and stay on point when it comes to fulfilling the purpose of your life. I hear you are a salesman?"

"Yes, sir, that's what I've been doing."

"So, you need to plan your sales calls, possibly schedule around new product releases, fit in additional training—but you'll always be up against other people who are working to be successful in the same type of business you're in. Fortunately, you will have access to the same amount of time each day that they do. So, it will be those who use and make the most of those minutes who have the best chance at accomplishment and fulfillment as a salesman."

Mr. Schilling was on a roll now. "If you don't have that plan, if you don't know where you are going and what you are working to accomplish, chaos will surely take over. Then, sadly, you will become part of someone else's plan. Now, hear me when I say this, because people disagree with me. I personally believe that you cannot manage time—it can't be done. Instead, you can manage yourself within time. I know, it seems like a trick, but I've been through the same training as you, and it's my belief system."

He continued, "There's also what some businesspeople refer to as the 80/20 rule, and it really affects your time. The thinking is that you will get 80 percent of your business from 20 percent of your customers. Now, that doesn't mean you should ignore the other 80 percent. Because over time those customers may change. You may lose a customer for several reasons: a poor economy, your competitor may win the account, or because of personnel changes that you can't control. So you must always continue to call on your entire customer base. But you need to be aware that some of them will want to monopolize your time with unproductive tasks that don't make you or the company any profit."

He picked up a book. "Sometimes I find great treasures in the weirdest places. I was at a garage sale combing through the tables when I saw this book. I thought, what a curious title, *Juggling Elephants*. I bought it for a quarter and read it the same night. Of course I already had a familiarity with time—I'm constantly surrounded by it, for goodness sake. But, believe it or not, this little book changed my whole life around when it comes to investing my time. Yes, you heard me correctly: I said investing rather than spending. It was a small distinction that helped me make the shift I needed to achieve everything I wanted for my own life.

"There are many other useful books worth reading, and I recommend you continue to feed and nourish your mind. I found that the thirty minutes in the evening I used to spend watching the local news was better spent reading a helpful book. The news seemed to be about the same every day, except for sports and weather. The main stories all seemed to be about shootings, accidents, and corrupt politicians. I found those stories didn't bring any lasting value to my life, and I can get the weather or sports report immediately on my computer or phone. I also realized that I only had a finite amount of time."

Thomas chuckled, "It's funny that you say that. I haven't even turned on my television in over a week."

Mr. Schilling handed the book to Thomas. "I'd like you to have this. Invest in yourself and reorganize what you do with your time, because it's so precious and needs to be monitored. I think it's the most valuable thing anyone has. Well—besides maybe air, food, and water."

Thomas accepted the book. "Thank you for the gift. I will read and cherish it."

"You are most welcome. The thing about money is, you can lose it all and start making more, but time—well, I have probably said it enough today: once it's gone, you can never get it back." He pointed to the book. "It's like juggling elephants—you just can't do it." The two laughed.

Thomas asked, "What do you do about those people in your life who don't or won't learn this lesson? For instance, a boss, an employee, a family member—even a spouse."

Mr. Schilling spread his feet and leaned on his desk. "It's really funny—people who like to waste time usually never want to do it alone. They get other people to join in." He looked toward the ceiling. "I guess that didn't really answer your question. How about this: 'If you are on task and fulfilling your purpose, you will know where to invest that time.'"

"I guess that's the bottom line—the question I need to answer, isn't it? Even though that was yesterday's lesson, I can see now why Tonya said she felt like it was the most important topic."

"Let's do a quick calculation," Mr. Schilling continued. "If you spend eight hours sleeping, eight more at work, add one for lunch, and a half hour commute each way, that's a thousand and eighty minutes alone. Now, as you know, most people don't work just eight hours, and if you live in a city like Los Angeles, you can triple that commute time. What if you tried to fit in a round of golf that day?"

Thomas made a sour face. "That would be at least another four hours, probably more."

"So, at the end of it all you'd be out of time for the day. Now, like I said before, you have the same amount of time as anyone else. It's what you do with it that matters. So, as you will find if you read the book I gave you—"

"*When* I read the book," Thomas interrupted.

Mr. Schilling smiled. "One way to win this battle against time misused is to plan out the important things first. If the events don't support your purpose, enhance your health, improve your relationships, or educate you in some way, then you shouldn't invest time in them. So, if you plan accordingly, you'll get to where you don't waste time on unimportant things."

The cuckoo clock chimed again and Mr. Schilling said, "Well, I am hopeful this has been a wise investment of our time. But that, my friend, is yet to be determined. I will leave you with one last thing, and then, unfortunately, I have somewhere else I need to be. Please do not look at life as a race to run. Your life should never be hurried through. Instead, look at it as a journey to be experienced, and you get to decide what adventures to have." Thomas gave an understanding nod.

"There is one more thing I could add," said Mr. Schilling, raising his eyebrows. "Make sure you respect other people's time. They may never have been introduced to the lesson you learned here today."

The two men rose and shook hands. "Thank you for your time," Thomas said warmly. "That phrase actually means something very different to me now because of you and this lesson. I will invest my time wisely from now on and will always respect everyone else's."

He made his way out of the store. As he got ready to climb in the car, he took one more look at the enormous clock above the building. He knew he would never look at time the same way again.

CHAPTER 11

All our dreams can come true, if we have the courage to pursue them.

—Walt Disney

Dream Big—I Triple Dog Dare You!

Thomas was sitting in bed thinking about his life and listening to the clock tick. He thought about the lesson Mr. Schilling had taught him as he rose, got ready, and met the car outside.

After a relaxing ride, he arrived at a building with a sign that read, THE SENSATIONAL GROUP. He was so excited that he leaped from the car and ran to the front door. He entered the building and was greeted by a beautiful young woman in a bright red dress.

"Welcome Thomas, I'm Angelica. Can I get you anything? A muffin, water, coffee?"

"No, thank you."

"Then why don't you follow me. Mr. Wallace is waiting for you in the garden." Thomas thought, *The garden?* The building was five stories high, with a large open-air atrium in the middle. All the walls that faced the inside of the atrium were made of glass, so everyone had a full view of each other, as well as the beautiful garden.

Angelica opened a glass door leading into the atrium and called out, "Mr. Wallace?"

There was a rustling of some bushes, and out popped a blond, blue- eyed man with a tablet and a bunch of crayons. "Hello, Thomas, I am Mr. Wallace, but please call me Karl. I have heard a great deal about you."

Angelica said, "If you don't need me any further, I'll go back up to my desk."

"Thank you, I've got him now." Karl said. "Please follow me." He turned and headed back into the bushes and Thomas followed.

Suddenly they came upon a koi pond with huge fish swimming about and a waterfall on one end. Thomas looked at it in amazement. Karl set his things down, put his hand in the water, and tried to pet one of the fish. "They are so beautiful. I wish I could swim like that."

"I do too. I swam all the time as a kid, but I can't remember the last time I went swimming."

"We can go later if you want."

Thomas looked puzzled for a second and pointed to the pond. "You mean in there?"

Karl laughed. "No, silly, in a pool. There is one at the YMCA a couple of blocks from here."

Thomas hesitated. "Thanks for the offer. Perhaps next time—I didn't bring my suit."

Karl reached down to try to pet the fish again. "Your choice— we can always get you one."

Thomas shook his head no. "I'm just fine right here—that is, if that's what you have planned for us."

"Well, we've got a field trip in a little bit. Is that okay with you?"

Thomas thought for a second and wondered if this could be a follow-up test about how to spend your time. He decided that he was surely in good hands and this is where he was supposed to be. He would invest his time in whatever activity Karl deemed suitable. "I'm fine with whatever you decide is best for me," he replied.

The fish were now swarming around Karl's hand. He stared blankly into the water. "As a child, I read everything I could. I was the kid at the library who checked out the maximum number of books allowed. I won all the reading awards and would pore through them by staying up past my bedtime with a flashlight. Looking back, there's no doubt that's what put me on my current path. I had such a wild imagination that every one of my teachers called me a daydreamer." Thomas moved closer to see the fish. Noticing this, Karl said, "Don't be shy, get in here and make some friends." Thomas put his hand in the water but still gave Karl his attention as he continued, "My folks would come to parent-teacher conferences and would hear how all I did in class was stare out the window. At recess I would lie in the grass and watch the clouds go by. I imagined that I was floating on top of them, and then that I was an astronaut flying up through them on my way to Mars."

Thomas said, "I was pretty much the same way."

Karl turned to him quickly. "So, are you still a dreamer?"

"I guess the dreamer in me got lost somewhere along the way as I grew up."

Karl got up, wiped his wet hand on his pants, and grabbed his things. "Follow me." Thomas shook the water from his hands and headed through the bushes behind him. "As you know, you're here to learn a lesson, one that will help you to be a better salesman." He chuckled. "Which is always interesting, because almost all the other mentors have a history of selling and I don't." Thomas was puzzled at this. Karl continued, "Like I said, I'm a dreamer. Growing up, everyone said it was a problem, because I never followed through on anything. Then along came Brad, and for the first time in my life, I felt understood and accepted. He just let me dream, and had someone else take care of the rest." He stopped, turned to Thomas, and flashed a smile.

The two made their way through a door, down a hall, and into Karl's office. It wasn't like any office Thomas had seen before. There was a desk, but it was covered with books, loose papers, maps, electronic parts, and clothing; there were a couple of beanbags, a movie projector, and a large screen. To Thomas, it looked more like a jam-packed, unorganized, thrift shop. Karl removed a few items from a chair and offered it to Thomas. "Have a seat." Thomas sat down, still amazed at the surroundings. Karl said, "It was funny how I got the job. I had been working at the hospital as a janitor when Brad and Harold Lancaster came by me in the hallway. I heard them complaining about the battery pack on his wheelchair running out of juice several times a day. So that night I went home and came up with a way to charge the batteries using a solar panel. I wrote everything on a napkin and the next time I saw them again, I gave it to Brad." Thomas had a look of total surprise on his face.

Karl continued, "Some people look at me as an inventor; they would probably say I need to protect my ideas, so I can make money from them. Well, I didn't do it to make money. I wanted that man not to have to worry about his wheelchair battery going dead at the wrong time or place. So, I dreamed up a solution. Well, at least I thought it would work. I'm not a licensed engineer, but I read books about electronics, manufacturing, civil and architectural engineering, and anything else that might help me with the creative process. Just a few weeks after I gave the napkin to Brad, he showed up at the hospital with a working prototype and offered me this job. Been here ever since."

"So, it sounds like you have a pretty cool job."

"The coolest. I can support anyone at any time. When someone in any of the companies or departments is having an issue, they call me. But I didn't start out in this position. It took a while before Brad came up with it. At first I helped on the wheelchair project, and that turned into a decent profit center for us."

"I'll bet there are tons of people facing the same problem," Thomas observed.

Karl went on, "Brad and I spent a lot of time talking initially and he said he was creating this position for me, because I had a way of looking at things that was still childlike, fresh, and unique. So many times people can't see a solution, because they've simply stopped dreaming. I, on the other hand, haven't. I use the critical thinking skills I've acquired, read voraciously, and continue to believe anything is possible. That's why I have been able to bring value.

"I'm totally free and I'm never limited by what other people might think or say. Brad and I share the belief that if someone can dream it up, it can become a reality. I am allowed to let my mind run wild. And the kicker is, I get paid to do it. It's fantastic to know the entire company is supportive and will encourage me to get in my creative mode and just dream stuff up. Then I hand it off to other people who work to make it happen. Sometimes if research and development gets stuck, they'll get me involved. Believe it or not, I'm never criticized for any idea—I actually don't know what happens to most of them. Once in a while, I get invited to the launching of a new product, or something I dreamed up wins an award and I am credited."

"Well, I'm guessing there are not a lot of openings in your department," Thomas joked.

Karl giggled. "No, you are right about that. Someone around here has to do some real work. Although I will need a replacement someday, and we did talk once about expanding the staff."

Refocusing, he continued, "To be successful, at least for what I do, you have to let go of what you think you know and allow your mind to go where it wants. It is the limiting of one's own mind that keeps a person from achieving greatness. We tend to think with filters and restrictions when we get older. That's why I enjoy being around children. Most of them still believe anything is possible—that's a great place to start when facing a challenge in your business or life. The question is, can you get yourself to believe it? Fortunately, I do!" He grabbed a small nerf basketball and, without looking, tossed it over his shoulder and made the basket. Thomas stared in amazement as though he had just seen a magic trick.

Karl picked up his shoulder bag. "So it is time for that little field trip. You still interested?"

Thomas nodded. "Of course. Do I need anything special?"

"No, we won't be gone very long."

As they walked toward the entrance, Karl said, "There's no doubt my success has come because I tend to dream bigger than most people. I've been able to do that because I've been surrounded with dream supporters, not dream killers, my entire life. Unfortunately, there are many more of the killers in the world."

They exited the building and jumped into the car that had been waiting for Thomas.

The driver sat waiting for instructions as Karl continued, "Keep in mind, these dream killers, they want to tell you all the reasons why you can't achieve something. They'll say you should 'come back to reality' and 'get your head out of the clouds.' So it's really simple: I just stay clear of anyone who acts or talks like that. Now, trust me, I understand you live in the real world, and so do I. But I believe that you make your own reality. I'm sure you have already been introduced to the idea that it's not what happens to you in life that matters, it's how you respond to it? I take full responsibility for where I'm at in my life. I'm well aware that I am who I am because of decisions I have made—not anyone else."

Karl gave instructions to the driver and sat back. "Have you ever watched the television show *Star Trek*?"

"Well, I've never seen the old television show, but I have seen all the newer movies."

Karl pulled out his cell phone and held it up. "The guy who dreamed up that original television show, Gene Roddenberry, brought us this." Thomas was keenly interested to hear this. "Think about computers, tablets, wireless earpieces—so many technologies he imagined or dreamed up: now they're real. That guy was a true visionary. He didn't care if people thought any of that technology was possible, or would ever be used in society, he just dreamed it up to make the show better."

Thomas glanced out the window and noticed they seemed to be pulling into the parking lot of the school where Sandy taught. He found himself becoming unusually nervous as the car came to a stop and they got out. Karl led them into the front office, where they signed in and received name badges. All the women knew Karl and treated them both very well. They made their way past the cafeteria, down a hall, and stopped outside a classroom. Thomas was sweating and wondering what was about to happen. Karl knocked and the two men entered. A woman in her sixties stood and announced, "It's Karl, and he's brought a friend." The children in the classroom erupted with cheers. It appeared to be a third- or fourth-grade class. They were still young, but you could tell they were engaged, and judging by the room decorations, fairly advanced students.

Thomas couldn't believe how much love and admiration these children were showing Karl. He was also relieved, because Sandy was nowhere in sight. It wasn't that Thomas didn't miss her, but he wasn't prepared to handle seeing her just yet. The entire classroom made their way over to an open area where there were lots of pillows. They all sat down and made themselves comfortable. Thomas was the last to sit, and Karl had to motion for him to join in. Karl set the bag he had brought in the center of the group and turned to Thomas. "This should be very interesting and a lot of fun."

The teacher quieted the group. "Now, let's all remember our manners. Mr. Karl doesn't have a lot of time today, so please, no one interrupt."

Karl motioned to the children. "Let's see, who will be first?" Every child's arm went in the air. He examined each child's face before pointing to a little red-haired girl. "Rebekah, today's your lucky day. Are you ready?"

She stood proudly. "Ready."

"You know the drill: name something in the bag."

The children all began shouting different answers as Rebekah stared intensely at the bag. The teacher shushed the children as Rebekah settled on her answer. "I think you brought a pony." Thomas was puzzled by the girl's response. He wondered what would make her give that answer. Karl peeked in the bag, then reached in and pulled out a toy pony. The girl shrieked with excitement. "I got it right, it's a pony!" She took the pony and went to sit down. Thomas looked on in amazement.

Karl looked around the room and pointed to a quiet boy. "Come on up here, you're next." The boy rose and came forward. "So, what else do you think I have in this bag? Something you want perhaps?" The boy looked sad, and shook his head with resistance.

The teacher chimed in, "Go ahead, it's okay."

The boy said shyly, "I know what I want isn't in there. It's impossible."

"Oh, now, nothing's impossible," the teacher replied. "Give it a try."

Karl nodded in agreement. The boy mumbled sadly, "My father."

Karl looked very serious. Thomas leaned forward to see how this would end.

"So, why do you hope I have your father in this bag?"

The boy answered, "Because he's away in the army and I haven't seen him in a long time."

Karl looked deeply at the boy. "Well, let's just see what's in here." He searched the bag with his hands and looked inside. Finally, he pulled out a laptop computer, opened it, and began pecking away on the keys. The boy slumped with sadness as everyone in the room sat quietly with anticipation. The teacher smiled from ear to ear.

After a moment, the boy heard his father's voice. "*Hello, Son.*" His eyes widened and Karl turned the laptop around toward the boy, revealing his father's face. The children began clapping, and the boy was so overcome with joy he began to cry. The teacher stepped in and took the boy and computer to the other side of the classroom to give him privacy for his face time with his dad. Thomas sat in amazement.

Karl let Thomas pick the next few children for the exercise. Unfortunately, the magical bag didn't deliver everything that was requested, but it didn't dampen the children's spirits. Finally, Karl opened the bag and brought out a package of chocolate chip cookies. He opened the package and shared them with everyone in the room.

The boy finished spending time with his father, and all the children thanked Karl for coming. The pony, the laptop, and a few other items remained with the class as everyone said their goodbyes and left. The two men wore huge smiles and silently made their way back to the office.

Thomas sat dumbfounded in the car, trying to understand what just took place. Karl explained, "You see, I go there every week, and sometimes a child will ask for something I never would have thought to bring. Only rarely do they become disappointed when they find I don't have the item. But that doesn't keep them from continuing to dream and ask for those things week after week. I just have to remember what they asked for and bring those items at some point. So, when someone does get the item they were dreaming about, it reinforces for everyone else the importance of keeping their dream alive. Whatever they get stays in the class for all to share. The girl who picked the pony wanted that over a month ago. As for the boy who wanted his dad, we have known he's been struggling with his father's deployment for months, so we spoke to his mother and arranged the call. Pretty simple way to teach the lesson of never limiting your dreams."

"In most cases, adults would have asked for something logical. They would think about the size of the bag, the cost of an item, and if they had been told no before and then they probably wouldn't ask for the same thing again. We want those children to believe anything is possible and never give up on that dream. This exercise keeps me on my toes, because I have to be resourceful, I have to listen, and most of the time I resort to using my critical thinking skills to keep the momentum going week after week."

"I totally get it." Thomas said. "Because by the time most kids grow up, they are jaded and cynical. If you never came back or if they never won the guessing game, you'd become one of those dream killers you were talking about. But you keep them believing week after week. That's awesome." Karl smiled with deep satisfaction.

The car pulled up in front of the office building and the two men headed back to Karl's office. As they sat down, Karl said, "The trick in life is to move from the dream to some kind of action that makes it real. That's when the magic really happens. Never lose your dream, but you always need to be doing something to bring it to life. Most things start out as dreams. The reason they turn into something tangible, though, is because somebody did something about it—they took action."

"I've had so many dreams but never did anything to make them come true," Thomas observed.

Karl asked, "Have you started dreaming about sales? I mean, since you are working to become a salesman in this company."

Thomas had a thoughtful look. "As funny as it sounds, I haven't really had time. I've been trying to learn and focus on one lesson at a time."

Karl smiled. "Well, now it's time to dream, and I want you to dream *big*! No limitations. Just let your mind go. Do you promise me you'll do that?"

Thomas nodded. "Yes, sir. No question."

"Now, I'm a darn good dreamer and I also believe I'm a pretty decent critical thinker. But what you'll learn tomorrow will help you take what I do to the next level."

"Are you going to tell me what that lesson is?" Thomas asked eagerly.

Karl shook his head. "I have probably said too much already. My job was to get you to understand the importance of dreaming, which is something you're probably already doing at night."

"I dream a lot, but then again, I've had a lot of nightmares as well."

Karl laughed. "Haven't we all. But I'll give you a secret. You can shift your dreaming into overdrive, and put your brain to use coming up with all kinds of great ideas and solutions."

"And how is that?"

"By setting up your unconscious. Just before you go to sleep, focus on a thought, a problem, or something you would like your brain to work on. I tend to ask myself great questions just before dozing off."

"That's it?"

"That's it," Karl replied. "Your brain is the greatest computer ever created. If you pose a question, it will work to provide an answer. Always keep in mind, the quality of your answers depends on the quality of your questions. If you ask, 'Why can't I ever get things right?' your brain will work to give you every reason why you don't get things right. But if you ask, 'What do I need to do differently to get things right this time?" your brain will give you a totally different set of answers.

"But that's a discussion for another time. Unfortunately, I've got some projects that require me to dream. For now, just focus on the lesson of dreaming and the process will take care of the rest."

The two stood and shook hands. Thomas said, "Thank you very much. Today was incredible."

Karl responded humbly, "You are welcome. Now go out there and *dream big*!"

Thomas made his way to the car and daydreamed the entire way home.

After being dropped off at his home, Thomas went out to the mailbox and opened the lid to find it chock full. He had been so busy he had forgotten to check the mail. He noticed that most of it was junk mail or what seemed to be bills. He entered the house and set the pile on the table to deal with later. Then he went out to the backyard, got comfortable, and spent the rest of the evening watching the sunset and dreaming. Finally, after dark, he headed into the house, grabbed a bite to eat, and went to his bedroom. As he pulled the covers up, he looked over at the empty pillow next to him that was meant for his love. He sighed deeply. With overwhelming sadness, he tossed and turned until he finally drifted off to sleep.

CHAPTER 12

It is not enough to take steps, which may someday lead to a goal; each step must be itself a goal and a step likewise.
—Johann Wolfgang von Goethe

Goal Setting—Take It One Step at a Time

The sun shown brightly through the window and across Thomas's bed as he lay snoring under a heap of twisted blankets and pillows. Suddenly, he sat up in a panic and noticed the clock on his nightstand was blinking. The power must have gone out during the night and caused him to oversleep. He leaped out of bed and headed to get ready.

Just as he turned the shower off, he heard the doorbell ring. He rushed to answer it wrapped only in a towel, greeting the driver, "I'm so sorry, it'll just take me a few more minutes to get ready." The driver looked him up and down, shook his head, smiled, and said, "I'll be in the car. Do your best to hurry, please, so we're not late." Thomas ran off to get dressed, leaving the driver to close the door before heading to wait in the car.

He quickly dried off, dressed, locked up the house, and climbed into the limo. He noticed no one else with them. The driver revved the engine and they sped off in a hurry. Thomas felt embarrassed, because every other day he had been ready. For some reason, today he was feeling a bit overwhelmed and edgy, so he was happy to be alone in the backseat and would have some time to get his act together as they drove. Perhaps it was the topic of dreaming big, or the trip he had made to Sandy's school the day before, but whatever the reason, his mind was racing uncontrollably.

The car came to a halt in front of the Sensational Group office building, and before Thomas could reach for the handle, the door flung open. Standing on the curb, holding the door in one hand with an iPad in the other, was a tall brunette. She had a smile as wide as the Grand Canyon. "Good morning, Thomas, I'm Alyssa Montgomery. We will be spending the next few hours together."

Thomas exited the car. "Nice to meet you, Alyssa." She closed the door and led him into the building. Thomas nodded at the receptionist, who stood, smiled, and waved at the two while talking on her headset. He also glanced into the atrium as they walked down the hall, but he didn't see Karl.

Alyssa opened the door to an office, and the two entered. As Thomas looked around, he noticed it was the same size as Karl's but was decorated very differently. It was perfectly organized, with a place for everything and everything in its place. Alyssa pointed to a couch. "I apologize for the not-so-warm welcome; we are a little behind."

"Thomas grimaced. "My apologies, I overslept."

She nodded, "That happens to all of us. Let's sit and see if we can get back on schedule. So, you spent yesterday with Karl?" Thomas nodded and she continued, "He and I are kind of a one-two punch and I love working with him. As you now know, he creates dreams, and I—well, I set the goals that help make those dreams come true."

Thomas was impressed. "I'll bet that takes a great deal of organization."

"It does. Once I'm clear and understand the dream, the next step is to create a blueprint for the steps it will take to make that dream become a reality. That's what goals really are, steps to fulfilling dreams."

"That makes total sense."

"Unfortunately, some people don't flesh out the plan to fulfill their dream, and they get stuck going from step to step, without holding that bigger picture in mind. We work very hard on mixing short and long-term goals to fulfill the original vision. I like the exercise of comparing a dream to a large amount of time, like a day, or week, and then view each of the goals as the seconds, minutes, or hours that fill up that amount of time."

"You make is sound so simple," Thomas observed. "But I know it's probably very difficult."

Alyssa giggled. "If you've ever had a dream come true, you probably employed the habits of goal setting to make it happen. We've been very fortunate and have been able to take most of Karl's dreams and bring them to reality. To do that, we have to use steps that can be monitored and adjusted to get the desired results. The longer you're around, the more you'll hear me say, "You can't manage what you don't measure." So, we analyze everything, and continue making adjustments until we succeed."

"Now that I think about it, I've had lots of dreams that never came true, because I never made a plan—I guess they are still just dreams."

"Exactly," Alyssa said. "And they will always be dreams until you set the appropriate goals and work toward making your dreams become reality."

She stood. "So, think about this for a second. If your dream is to become a professional basketball player, you don't just show up and join an NBA team. You have to begin by accomplishing lots of smaller goals to move toward that end."

Thomas chuckled. "That's one dream I've never had. I know my limitations."

Alyssa laughed. "No matter how impossible the dream may seem in the beginning, there's an old saying that may help you when you are facing a big challenge." Thomas sat forward attentively. "How do you eat an elephant?" He looked puzzled and shrugged. She answered, "One bite at a time."

He grinned. "I guess when you look at it that way, I could probably accomplish almost anything with patience and a good plan. So, how did you come to join the team here?"

"Good question," she said, moving toward her bookshelves. She ran her fingers along the bindings of several books. "Probably like many of the other mentors you are meeting, I had a chance encounter with Brad."

Thomas sat forward with great interest. She began, "It was definitely a lowlight in my life. I had started dating a guy named Steve and we were at a gas station. He was fueling up and I went in to buy some things. When we got back into the car, he became angry because he thought I was flirting with the attendant. The situation quickly escalated and I got out of the car, which caused him to blow his top. He jumped out, came around, and slapped me. I was totally shocked—no one had ever done anything like that to me before. He was shouting and I was crying hysterically. The next thing I knew, Brad was standing between us telling Steve to calm down. In a flash, Steve got back in the car and drove off."

Thomas was incredulous. "You've got to be kidding."

Alyssa shook her head. "Nope. I was standing there and Brad was trying to comfort me. Once I settled down, he gave me a ride home. I don't know why I trusted him, I just did."

Thomas laughed. "That guy ought to start a taxi service."

She went on, "Well, one thing led to another and we became friends. Then, a couple of months later, I found myself in this position. Brad saw a need for my skill set and I've been with the company ever since."

Thomas smiled. "Brad sure has a way of turning bad situations into good ones."

"Like no one I've ever seen before," she said.

She refocused and moved closer to Thomas. "Have you ever heard of Dr. Edwards Deming?"

Thomas shook his head. "No, I can't say that I have."

124

She continued, "A great deal of what I know I learned from him. You've heard of Toyota Quality right?" Thomas nodded. "Well, Mr. Deming was the man who taught the Japanese about quality. He was an expert at breaking down systems and processes into the smallest details by using time and motion studies. By fully understanding his methods, I learned to take a project or one of Karl's dreams, determine every piece or goal that's needed to accomplish the mission, and perform each step correctly and efficiently."

Thomas cleared his throat. "So, how do you determine what pieces will be needed? I mean, where do you start?"

She continued, "Well, the rule is always to start with the end in mind."

"So a dream, and then you come in?"

She smiled and nodded. "That's about right. I've learned to see every part that will create the whole. I learned to do it with products, services, and procedures. For instance, if someone described a beautiful cake they wanted made, we would have to choose the flavors, colors, size, how it will be decorated, etc. Then, you'd determine what ingredients would be needed, what size cake pans, what size oven, how long to bake it, the temperature, and who can do the job. Fortunately, with something like a cake, there's usually an existing recipe to follow. And even if it's a proven winner, you can still put your own twist on it, and perhaps even improve on it."

"She went on, "To create success, I use a technique called modeling. It's where you find someone who has already achieved what you are searching for, and copy them."

Thomas interrupted, "Isn't that like cheating?"

She laughed. "Well, it is against the law to copy certain things, like trademarks or copyrighted material. But I'm talking about something different. If you saw someone successfully jump over a stream, you could copy them without any worry of the sheriff coming to arrest you." They both laughed and she added, "Simply put, if there was already a successful formula or pattern for accomplishing something, that's where I always begin. I mean, why reinvent the wheel."

Thomas nodded in agreement. "That makes sense, I just wasn't thinking like that."

"I begin by assessing the person's skills and talents, and I also make sure I have a deep understanding of their belief system."

Thomas looked puzzled. "Their belief system?"

She wrinkled her forehead. "If I'm correct, you've already had that lesson—what a person believes makes a huge difference in whether they can or will achieve something."

"Very true. That's why I'm still being mentored."

Alyssa giggled, "Don't worry about it. I'm sure your brain is probably on overload by now."

Thomas sat up straight. "Keep it coming—I want to learn everything."

"Great. So if you can't find someone who has accomplished exactly what you want, then look for a similar success story that you can mimic."

"What if there's no successful template to mimic?"

She chuckled. "That's when my juices really begin to flow. Something I find quite often is that people set a goal, they achieve it, but then that's the end of it."

"I'm not sure what you mean."

She went on, "The goals they set aren't part of a bigger plan or picture, so they gain some momentum by accomplishing a goal, but they haven't looked ahead to see what it means. For instance, as a salesperson you make it a goal to get a business card from every person you meet. After a while, you have a whole Rolodex full of business cards, but what was the point?"

"But if I had collected all those business cards as a part of a bigger plan to increase my territory by following up and selling more, then that would make sense."

She clapped her hands. "Exactly! Each goal should have a purpose and it should build on the previous goal. They are a means to an end." She beamed with excitement. "Do you have a dream you want to accomplish, but haven't figured out how to do it yet?"

"Yes."

"Do you mind sharing it with me?"

Thomas looked a bit embarrassed, but he answered, "Well, now that I have this opportunity, I want to be the greatest salesman this company has ever had."

She raised her eyebrows. "That's a great response. You've certainly got the end in mind. Now, I must ask, do you believe you can do it?"

Thomas answered firmly, "I will say that with every new skill I learn, I gain more confidence. So yes, I believe that when I'm done with my training, I'll have the tools to go out and make that dream come true."

Alyssa sat back with a grin. "So now all we have to do is figure out which company you'll be placed in or what product you'll be selling, and we can create a plan for your success."

"By setting up my goals, right?"

She laughed. "Precisely!"

"Let's do a quick exercise," she suggested. "Hypothetically, if the Sensational Group owned a paper towel company and you were brought in to take over sales, where would you begin?"

Thomas took a long pause to gather his thoughts. "I think I'd start with the existing accounts. I'd ensure that those relationships were sound, and then I would make a list of target customers."

"Who would you target? Would you go by size, geography, or maybe customers who had switched to a competitor?" He looked stuck. She squinted and said, "I was purposely trying to mislead you. Now let's put you back on track. Remember, start with the end in mind. What would sales success look like in your mind?"

Thomas closed his eyes tightly, thought for a minute, and then began to speak. "I could see myself selling paper towels to every customer in the city. The orders piling up, the phones ringing off the wall, trucks loading out around the clock, and a warehouse that was as busy as Grand Central Station. No matter how big or small the account, I'd be their salesman." He paused and she encouraged him to continue. "Heck, it would cause the competition to close their doors and leave town. Places of business that had hand blowers in their bathrooms would yank them off the wall and put up paper towel dispensers, and at the end of the year I'd be standing at a sales meeting receiving an award." With his eyes still closed, he smiled and put his arms up in victory.

Alyssa clapped her hands. "Now that's what I call a dream."

Thomas slumped in his seat. "But I bet most people would say that I'm not very realistic."

Alyssa stood, stamped the ground, and raised a fist at Thomas. "Who cares what they say? This is your dream, and that's where all great success stories begin. So, if this were a real opportunity, you created a great dream, and then we would begin to develop goals to make that dream come true. That's all that matters. That's the way the system works."

Thomas apologized sheepishly. "I'm sorry, I didn't mean to upset you."

"Just stick with what you've learned and trust the system," she replied. "It's been proven to work over and over. Now, I know that was just an exercise, but you have to be committed. Do you understand?"

Thomas nodded. "Yes, again I apologize. I'll get it down, I promise."

She pointed her finger and closed one eye, "Your dream has to be defined, fixed, and you have to be able to see it clearly at all times. Imagine a target—you know, a bull's eye. Now, you—you're the expert marksman and someone has just handed you a rifle you aren't familiar with. You aim, shoot, and determine where the bullet hit. If it didn't hit the center, you adjust and shoot again. A great marksman would do this over and over until he gets the desired result. That's how you will become that great salesman. You'll keep your dream or target in clear sight, and keep adjusting your goals until you hit that bull's eye. Now, if you don't believe you can ever hit the bull's eye, we have a different set of problems."

Thomas chirped, "No, I'm sure I will inevitably hit it, and once I learn how, I'll do it every time."

Alyssa offered her hand for a high five. "That's what I'm talking about!"

He slapped her hand. "So, I guess once I know my job, I'll spend some time dreaming, get with you on my goals or steps, and then I'll be off to the races?"

Alyssa laughed. "Now you've got it. Once we know where you are placed in the company, we will spend another day together formulating your goals."

She glanced at her watch, "Well, unfortunately our time today has come to an end."

They stood and shook hands. "Thanks very much," Thomas said warmly. "I've learned a lot and I'll be ready to come back soon and set my goals."

"I look forward to it." She opened the door.

Thomas said, "I can find my way out, and maybe I'll see Karl."

Alyssa smiled. "If you do, tell him I said hello."

As Thomas exited and headed to the lobby area, he looked for Karl. He didn't see him, but he did wave to the receptionist before stepping outside to meet the driver. They climbed into the car and headed home.

The ride seemed shorter than normal. As the driver reached Thomas's neighborhood, he said, "I apologize, but I'm not sure what tomorrow's schedule is yet. The mentor you are scheduled to meet with hasn't provided the final details, so it could be anytime tomorrow."

Thomas smiled. "It's not a problem, I don't have anything else to do right now. I'll be up and ready for anything that comes my way."

The driver laughed deeply and said with a smile, "Let's hope so, sir."

The car pulled into the driveway and the driver opened the door for Thomas to get out. They shook hands and Thomas quickly made his way into his house and closed the door for the night.

CHAPTER 13

===

Judge a man by his questions rather than his answers.

—Voltaire

If You Want a Better Answer, Ask a Better Question

It was still dark outside as Thomas leaned over and flipped the switch on his alarm clock before it had a chance to go off. He tossed the covers back, hopped out of bed, wiped the sleep from his eyes, and headed into the kitchen. After making some hot tea, he thought about the lesson he had learned the day before and wished he had been able to have Alyssa help him set some goals right then. Thomas noticed the still unopened pile of mail that he had put on the table. Seeing the bills made him anxious about his future. He was ready to get his new career started, and as he began to thumb through the stack, he wondered when he would begin earning a paycheck again. He stopped as he came across a small envelope with his name handwritten on the front, but without postage or a return address. He was curious who would have sent him this, since he was new to this address and very few people knew where he lived.

Sitting at the table, he tore into the mysterious offering. Inside he found one sheet of paper folded in thirds. He opened it and saw a large question mark drawn in the middle of the page. No name, no other notes or markings, just the symbol. Thomas took his tea out to the front porch to watch the sun come up and think about the note. Suddenly, he noticed someone had spray-painted a large white question mark on his front lawn, looking crisp and clean against the green grass. His curiosity now turned to frustration. He walked out to the street to view the mark from a different point, and glanced around the neighborhood to see if there was someone watching him. After a few minutes of investigation, he headed back into the house.

As Thomas made his way into the kitchen, he stopped in his tracks: it dawned on him that Brad was probably involved in this somehow. He didn't know what it meant, but he was sure the reason for the question marks would soon be revealed. A smile broke out across his face and a sudden calm came over him. With confidence, he headed to the shower to get ready for whatever was coming his way.

He had just returned to the front room when the doorbell rang. He quickly opened the door, expecting to find the driver, as usual. But, to his surprise, there was a real clown with a painted face, in full costume, carrying a backpack. Thomas had no idea who the person was, but he could tell it was a woman under all the makeup and costume. She had a smile that would make even a hardened criminal laugh, but it was creepy how she stood perfectly still and said nothing. Thomas giggled and looked past the clown for the limo or the driver, but they were nowhere to be found.

"So, are you here for work or for fun?" he asked. The clown continued to stand motionless. Thomas began to feel very uncomfortable. Although the clown had a huge painted grin on her face, the situation didn't seem funny at all.

Thomas stuck his hand out to shake and introduced himself. "Well, then, hello. I'm Thomas." The clown continued to stand and stare. Thomas was at a lost for how to interpret the situation, but in his gut he figured this was some kind of test. He steadied himself to play along with the clown. "Welcome to my home—would you please come in?"

This time, to his surprise, the clown nodded yes, honked a little horn on her belt, and entered. Thomas shut the door and turned to find the clown standing menacingly close. There was a moment of awkwardness as he stepped back and mumbled, "Well, this is going to be interesting." He sat down and motioned for the clown to join him. She stood as rigid as a statue. Thomas pleaded, "Will you please come have a seat?" The clown smiled a big smile and sat down beside him.

Thomas pondered the situation for a moment. "So, you respond to certain things I say, but not others." He chuckled. "I never said Simon says—so what's the catch?" Then he noticed a small pin in the shape of a question mark attached to the clown's shirt. "Aha— you are the one who sent me the note and painted the question mark on my lawn." The clown grinned from ear to ear. Thomas wrinkled his forehead in thought. "So what does all this mean? Question mark, question mark, what are you trying to teach me?" The clown nodded as though Thomas might be on to something. He stood, put his hands behind his back, and began to pace around the room. The clown made a motion as though she needed to use the restroom. Thomas said, "Do you need to use the bathroom?" The clown nodded. He took a couple of steps toward the hallway and pointed. "It's the first door on the left." She took her backpack and disappeared down the hall.

Thomas picked up the note and took another long look. Then he returned to the couch to try to solve the riddle. Within a few minutes, he heard the bathroom door open and footsteps coming back into the living room. Before he could look up the clown said, "It sounded a lot funnier when Brad and I discussed this last week." Thomas turned to find the clown had stripped the wig and makeup off while in the bathroom and was now out of character. Without the disguise, he could see her reddish-blond hair, light skin, freckles, and blue eyes. Definitely the features of a true Irish woman, he thought. He rose and reached to shake hands. "Well, I guess you know I'm Thomas, nice to meet you again."

"How do you do, Thomas, my name is Laura Newman."

Thomas waited for her to sit first and then sat down. "I've been learning a lot of lessons since I started this journey, but none of them have been this ..."

"Bizarre?" she offered.

He laughed. "Well, I guess that's one way to describe it."

"Hopefully it will all make sense by the time we are through today," she said with a chuckle. She set her backpack on the ground and began, "So, as you can guess, I'm one of your mentors. Do you have any idea what my topic might be?"

Thomas looked skyward. "Well, I figure it has something to do with all the question marks that have popped up around my home and on your clothing."

"You are on the right track for sure."

He thought for a moment but soon lost patience. "Is there any chance you'll just tell me the topic instead of me guessing?"

She quickly answered, "Yes."

He frowned. "So, when will you tell me?"

"As soon as you ask me."

The exercise was beginning to dawn on Thomas. With a different demeanor, he said, "Ms. Laura, would you please go ahead and share with me now the topic you are here to teach me today?"

She smiled and clapped her hands. "Why, yes, Thomas, I would be happy to." She began by pointing to the pin on her blouse. "I used the question mark symbol, because the lesson I am here to teach you is this:"—she paused for dramatic effect—"If you want a better answer, ask a better question." She waited for Thomas to soak it in. After a long pause, she went on, "Today will be a simple introduction to that topic, probably like most of your other meetings with mentors." Reaching into her backpack, she pulled out a book and handed it to Thomas. "This is for you. It should tell you everything you ever wanted to know about questions."

He accepted the book with both hands respectfully and said, "Thank you! I'll use and cherish this."

"Hopefully you will find it helpful as you continue on your journey."

Thomas flipped the book over and was surprised to see a picture of Laura with her name. "Wow—this is your book?"

"Well, not just mine. I'm the coauthor. It was recently released. It was a project that was a couple of years in the making." Thomas opened the book to find an inscription and read it aloud: "Thomas— every answer you will ever need can be yours, if you simply learn to ask a better question. All the best, Laura."

Thomas closed the book. "Okay, without sounding rude, what does this have to do with a clown?"

Laura replied with a belly laugh. "Well, I was attempting to teach you the lesson in a fun way, but it didn't work out as well as I had hoped. I'm a professional clown, and I was only going to respond to your direct commands in a nonverbal way, and only if you asked a good question." Thomas raised his eyebrows, beginning to understand. "When you first asked me if I was here for fun or work, I didn't answer. I was hoping you would figure it out and ask a better question. If you had asked independent questions about whether I was here for work or fun, I could have nodded yes. That's why when you asked me to come in, I did."

He smiled. "I guess I just wasn't catching on."

"It's not your fault, I probably should have asked some better questions before trying that new idea out on you. I've never delivered the content that way before."

Thomas motioned toward the kitchen. "Would you like something to drink, or a snack?"

Laura shook her head. "No, thank you, but I appreciate the offer. I want to go ahead and quickly cover some things, because I'll need to leave in a little while. I'm heading to the children's hospital this afternoon to spread some cheer." Thomas smiled at the thought.

With a more serious look on her face, Laura said, "I've been told you want to be a sensational salesman."

"Without sounding cocky or arrogant," Thomas replied, "I'm *going* to be a sensational salesman."

Laura grinned. "I like that attitude. Well, in order to stay ahead of the competition, you are going to have to learn to ask better questions. Sometimes, neither you nor the people you are going to deal with or attempt to serve will know the answers, and that's why asking a better question will be so important."

"Just a moment, if you don't mind," Thomas said, rising, "I want to grab my journal to make notes. I want to capture everything. I know it's probably in the book, but this will help me speed up the learning process."

He returned and she continued, "First, think about how a person learns. Sure, there are times when a question isn't involved. They could learn through experience, happenstance, or by a number of other ways. But discovery, invention, and even basic change usually come from someone asking a question. In school, most of us were taught to ask who, when, why, what, where, and how questions. But the great intellectuals who moved mankind forward learned to ask different, better questions. They asked questions no one else had thought of." Thomas sat listening with great interest.

"When you begin to read that book, you'll find there are more categories of questions than you ever could have imagined. There are internal questions, the ones you ask in your head, like *Why can't anything good ever happen to me?* You will find that that particular question is also a disempowering question—the opposite of an empowering question." Thomas had a focused look and was trying to keep up. He could tell Laura was truly passionate about this topic. "You see," she continued, "if you pose a question to yourself, your brain will work until it can provide an answer, just like a computer. If you ask poor or disempowering questions, your brain will probably give you poor answers. So, with the question I asked earlier, *Why can't anything good ever happen to me?* it would work to provide you all the reasons why nothing good ever happens to you. But if you ask a better question, like *What do I need to adjust in my life so that whatever happens is good?* your brain will work to find answers to that question." Thomas looked as though he had had an "aha" moment. "I totally get that: it's like 'garbage in, garbage out.' I think Karl started to tell me something about this, but then stopped and said I would learn it later."

Laura laughed. "Karl, huh. Well, I'll forgive him. He's actually one of the best I've ever met at asking better questions. It probably has to do with how he thinks. I mean, he lives a life with no limitations. He truly believes anything is possible, so he continues asking better questions until he gets what he wants. In fact, that's one of the marks of a person who has achieved anything great in life. They keep going until they find a way. Any change in business or in life usually comes from a different way of thinking, which really means a different set of questions." Thomas looked stumped. She went on, "Go ahead and test the idea. If you want to improve a product, what would you do?"

Thomas thought for a second. "I guess you are right—I'd have to ask some kind of question. How can this be better, what does my customer need, how can we make it cheaper?"

Laura rocked back in her seat with excitement. "Here's another fun exercise: try going for a specified length of time without asking a question, regardless of whether it's in your own mind or out loud."

"How long?" Thomas blurted.

She laughed loudly. "See—that was just a few seconds."

Thomas rolled his eyes. "Okay, you got me."

Laura went on, "Have you ever had someone start a conversation with you by saying, "Can I ask you a question?"

"Sure, all the time."

"Well, isn't that ridiculous? As soon as they said that, they asked a question." They sat silently for a second as Thomas registered the point. "I like to respond with, *"You just did, but would you like to ask another?"* And notice: even my response is a question. Believe it or not, I've tried to go a whole day without asking a question."

"Did you make it?"

"Unfortunately, no. Even though I had almost no contact with anyone, I found myself silently asking questions in my own head. Remember, I called those internal questions."

Thomas sat back. "Thinking about it, I can see how it would be almost impossible not to ask questions throughout the day. So, if you don't know how to ask good ones, it could keep you from becoming truly successful."

"Correct, and not only in business, but in life."

"I can attest to that," Thomas asserted. "I'm sure that if I had asked better questions at several key times in my life, things would be a lot different."

"Let's focus on the business side of things for a minute," Laura interjected. "There are people who provide sales training, and during that training they teach you to ask what are called open-ended questions. This is to keep the communication with the customer flowing. They want you to stay away from eliciting one-word answers, like no. If you were my salesperson at a store, you wouldn't want to ask if I needed help, because I could easily say no—thereby ending the conversation. Then what would you do? Of course, there are salespeople in every industry who go straight to the old standby, 'Do you have any questions?' Again, the potential customer can easily say no. There may be a time when you ask, 'Do you have any additional questions?' but you don't open with that one. So, I've found that with a little creativity, you can formulate better questions that help or provide genuine value to a customer and allow for continued communication. Because, in sales, you really need to get *answers* to determine what a potential customer or client needs or wants, so you can help them."

Thomas quickly jotted down some notes and said, "I can attest that in the past I approached thousands of potential customers with bad questions."

"Like?"

"Like something as simple as, 'Can I stop by when I'm in your area?' What a dumb question, knowing what I know now." This made Laura laugh. "Looking back, what if I had made just a slight change and asked, 'Would you like to meet with a supplier who would treat you like you were the only customer in the world?'"

"Hey, that's pretty good," Laura said with enthusiasm. "And, by the way, you asked another question before you changed the first question."

They both laughed together. Thomas said, "Until you pointed it out, I wouldn't have believed how many poor questions I ask, but how much better they could be with just a little thought or a change of habit."

"Which in turn would give you better answers," Laura pressed on, "which is what most people are searching for when they begin asking questions. I've trained lots of sales people, and one of the first exercises I have them work on is the list of twenty."

Thomas asked, "The list of twenty?"

"The list of twenty is simple. You create twenty questions that are specific to your industry and that pertain to your customers—questions that they probably have never been asked by another salesperson before."

"That's genius," Thomas said.

"Thank you. It has provided some incredible results."

"Can you share some examples of the questions?"

Laura looked at the ceiling and replied, "Yes." Then she sat silent.

Thomas rolled his eyes. "*Would* you please share some examples of questions from the exercise right now?"

Laura giggled. "You bet. One of my favorites was, 'What's the biggest challenge you face that you haven't been able to find a good solution for?' You see, even if the sales person doesn't have a product or service that solves the problem, the potential customer will realize that this person cares about their entire business—and who knows, if they do happen to solve that issue, what a strong business relationship they will have. By the way, it's also a question that's impossible to answer no to."

"I like it, keep them coming."

She thought for a second. "Another was, 'What issues or challenges have you had with vendors that you wish would go away?' Now, I've never seen a company that has perfect relationships with their vendors. This allows them a forum to share the problems, without necessarily throwing someone specific under the bus, and you'll find out what not to do if you get the chance to serve them."

Thomas said, "Those are better questions than 'What can I do to earn your business?'"

Laura smirked. "Yeah, that's just plain lazy. Most clients want to see what you are worth; they'd like to see you work to earn their business."

"Is it possible some of the questions you shared may catch a person off guard and make them feel uneasy?"

"That's definitely possible," Laura replied. "You'll have to see where they are in the process. If you go too heavy too early, they may think you are prying where you don't belong. Being able to ask those questions is much easier if the client believes you are there to help and they can trust you."

Thomas chuckled. "And they will begin to trust you as soon as they find out you are honest. Thinking about the question 'What issues or challenges have you had with vendors that you wish would go away?'—if they do share an answer, a salesperson would instantly know where and how to provide value. What a great surprise for them if you showed up with a solution—that would surely help to solidify a relationship."

"That's when your customer stickiness factor increases," Laura observed.

"Customer stickiness factor. I can't say that I've heard that phrase before."

"It's just as it sounds," Laura explained. "The closer the relationship you have with a customer, the stickier it gets and the harder to separate." She thought for a second. "Well, I guess some people may think it could also mean 'Things are getting sticky, or bad, with a customer,' but that's not how I mean it. Becoming sticky is about being close, sharing something, being a partner, and having a relationship that is so good and so intertwined that it's more difficult to switch vendors than it is to forgive you when something doesn't go well.

"I was taught in the past to look at myself as a tick, and to burrow deep into a customer so they can't get rid of me. I'm guessing you probably don't like that example?"

Laura frowned. "No, because if you think about it, a tick is happy about sucking blood, but the host doesn't get anything, except maybe Rocky Mountain spotted fever."

Thomas grimaced. "Good point."

Laura reached into her bag, pulled out a scrambled Rubik's cube, and handed it to Thomas. "Would you solve this for me right now please, and hand it back in one minute?"

Thomas stared at the cube for a second and began to frantically fumble with it. He quickly gave up in frustration. "Who am I kidding? I've never been able to figure these out."

Laura set it down beside him on the couch, then picked it up, began twisting and turning the pieces, and in short order had it solved. "This puzzle is just like a customer," she said quietly. "If you don't keep making adjustments or asking better questions, and learn the pattern for success, you won't ever make things totally right. Sure, you may get one side all the same color, but you won't complete it unless you invest the time and energy to finish the challenge."

Thomas looked embarrassed. "I have always been the guy trying to find shortcuts. When something required real hard work and follow-through, I usually didn't do well. The evidence is there. I'd either quit, or get fired."

Laura picked up the cube again. "So, let's think about the lessons you have learned so far, and the one you are learning today, and apply it to this situation."

Thomas sat up with a look of determination. "Okay. So, honesty—I don't know how to do this. Value and belief—it's important to succeed with this test for many reasons, and I believe anything is possible. Communication—*I will do this*. And as for our relationship—it's going to create a strong bond between you and me when I succeed because of your mentorship."

"That's the right idea," Laura interrupted, "but unfortunately we are going to have to end this session here. You keep the cube and do your best to solve it." She quickly scrambled the cube and handed it to Thomas.

Thomas stood up, staring at the Rubik's cube. "I'll ask the right questions when it comes to researching and completing this little challenge."

They moved toward the door. Laura said, "Thomas, though we had to cut today short, I'll do my best to make myself available if you need me." She smiled. "Just make sure you are ready with great questions." She stepped outside and walked to the waiting car.

The driver opened the door and called to Thomas, "Do you know how to solve those things?"

Thomas smiled. "Not yet, but I will shortly."

The driver closed the door and drove Laura away.

CHAPTER 14

Your brand is what other people say about you when you're not in the room.

—Jeff Bezos

Branding Isn't Just for Cattle

Thomas rolled over and struggled to sit up in bed. He had slept very heavily and would probably need a cold shower to help wake up. After a couple of minutes, he switched on the lamp and stared proudly at the perfectly completed Rubik's cube sitting beside his alarm clock. He was beginning to nod back off when he was startled by the *RING* of the doorbell. He leaped from the bed, put on a robe, and headed to see who was paying him such an early visit. He reached the door, peered through the peephole, and to his surprise spotted Brad standing on his front porch. Thomas opened the door and motioned him in. "Good morning, come in, come in."

"Good morning. Sorry for coming over unannounced—I know it's early. I would have called—"

"It's fine," Thomas assured him. He shut the door. "Can I get you something?"

"No, thanks. In fact, I came to take you to breakfast to meet up with another mentor."

Thomas fumbled with his robe. "How can I say no to breakfast and learning something new? Can you give me a few minutes to get ready?"

"Sure. Originally this was going to be a lunch, but the guy called late last night and asked to move it up. He has to go out of town and I wanted you to stay on track. I decided to come and get you rather than asking the driver at the last minute. I hope that was okay."

"Definitely. He yawned. "I'll hurry and get dressed."

Thirty minutes later, they were at the restaurant. The hostess knew Brad. "Good morning, Mr. Williams, right this way." They followed her toward a table in the back where a man was already seated. Thomas recognized him immediately: he was a celebrity around the city and his face and name could be seen everywhere. He had commercials, billboards, and a catchy jingle that ended with, *"Just call Robert Nigh, the Real Estate Guy."* As they arrived at the table, Robert rose to greet Brad with a warm smile and a handshake. "Brad, so nice to see you again. Sorry for the last-minute change."

"No worries—we're just glad you were still able to meet."

Robert turned to Thomas. "So, I take it you are Thomas?"

Thomas shook hands. "Yes, sir, it's a pleasure to meet you."

Brad added, "As you know, he's in training and has been a great student so far."

"So, how is that going? Learning a lot?"

Thomas replied, "I now realize how much I didn't know. Every day I learn something new."

"That's good to hear, I'm still learning every day as well—that's what keeps me ahead of the competition. And I can assure you that *change* will always be around the next corner, so it's a good practice to constantly feed your mind and continue learning new things."

"Thank you for that advice."

The waitress approached, efficiently took their drink order, and quickly slipped away.

Robert addressed Brad. "So, does he know the lesson for today?"

"No, I'd never steal your thunder," Brad replied. "This is your show, you do the honors."

Robert turned to Thomas. "I don't know about it being my show, but I'm excited to be in a position to share what I consider to be a very valuable lesson with you. Make no mistake, what I know about this subject isn't all originally mine; I've collected the best methods and practices from other successful people and used them whenever possible." Thomas sat forward with keen interest as Robert cleared his throat and continued, "My topic is branding."

"Well, it certainly seems like you have a great grasp of that subject," Thomas quipped. All three men laughed. Thomas reached in his pocket, pulled out a small pad and pen, and asked, "Do you mind if I take some notes?"

The two men seemed impressed and nodded in agreement. "By all means," Robert replied. "Whatever you miss we can go over again at another time, if need be. Let me start by saying there have been lots of people who deserve accolades for helping me get to where I am today. Although when it comes to my brand and my understanding of how to propel my name forward, I have to give the bulk of the credit to a man named Scott Ginsberg. Ever heard of him?"

Thomas shook his head no. "I can't say that I have."

Robert leaned forward and continued, "Scott is known to the world as the Nametag Guy and is considered to be the leading authority on branding and approachability. He's got a great story that started as he was finishing up college." The waitress brought their water, juice, and coffee and took their food order.

Robert went on, "As he was leaving a job fair, he saw a trash can filled with temporary nametags that the attendees were throwing away. He thought, *What could I do in this moment that would be different from everyone else?* He made the decision right then never to take his nametag off." He paused. "I mean never! Twenty-four hours a day, seven days a week, this guy wears a nametag that reads, HELLO, MY NAME IS SCOTT.

Thomas sat engrossed, with his mouth slightly open.

Robert went on, "Funny thing, though. This story isn't actually about his nametag—it's about him and his brand. He's written more than a dozen books, speaks all over the world, and you can bet his brand is sticky in more ways than one."

"So, he's a walking billboard?" Thomas said.

Robert nodded. "Yes, but more than that—he's a live billboard and he's very approachable, so he never meets a stranger and *everyone* remembers him by name. There's only one Scott, the Nametag Guy!"

He held his finger up and continued, "And there's only one Robert Nigh, the Real Estate Guy. Yes, I know I kind of copied him, but when someone gives you a successful recipe, you should just start cooking." The waitress and a helper returned with their breakfast. Robert moved the plates to the side, reached into a bag he had sitting beside the table, pulled out several books, placed them in front of Thomas, and said, "Here's a little something for you."

Thomas was taken aback and clearly thankful. He replied, "Thank you, that's very kind." He picked up a book and noticed that the author was Scott Ginsberg, with his picture on the cover. As he opened the book, he saw an inscription that read, "*Thomas, All the best and make sure you leave your own, unique mark on the world. Your friend, Scott.*" Thomas beamed with pleasure.

"Take advantage of the books," Robert advised. "There's a lot of great information in there."

"I'll put them to good use," Thomas assured him.

Brad pointed to the picture of Scott on the cover. "Perhaps someday you'll get the chance to meet him and hear him speak."

Robert added, "I remember the first time I met with him." He laughed. "It was funny, because I asked if I could pick his brain for a minute, and you know what his response was?" Thomas shook his head no and waited for the answer. "He said he was sorry that he couldn't let me pick it, but that he would certainly *rent it* to me. I thought that was genius." Thomas looked puzzled. Robert continued, "I mean it—he even has the website rentscottsbrain.com."

Robert took a bite and continued, "Just an incredible guy with a fantastic mind. And, if you ask the ladies, they'd say, "He's one smoking hot piece of brain candy." They all laughed.

Brad said, "I learned a great deal from Scott and Robert about enhancing my brand, and protecting it. It's important to understand that everything you do and say, as well as how you handle yourself and appear to others, will affect a brand—my brand—and yes, your brand."

"There's no question about that!" said Robert.

The waitress arrived to top off their drinks, and the conversation continued. Robert took a couple of quick bites and asked, "Do you know what the word *brand* really means?"

"Something recognizable?" Thomas offered.

Robert looked at Brad and smiled. "Okay, recognizable for what?"

Thomas didn't want to seem ignorant, but he didn't want to get in over his head. So he gave an honest response: "I don't really know the answer, but I would be grateful if you would educate me." There was a long pause at the table before Robert broke out in a giggle. "Boy, you are good." He turned to Brad, "He's good. How can I say no—of course I'll educate you. That's why we're here, right?

"Okay—there are several definitions, but I believe a brand is a promise to deliver a certain standard. Or sometimes, unfortunately, not deliver it. It notifies a potential customer of the level of service or the quality of the product they can expect to receive. It can be an intangible item, or something unique in the marketplace. Here's an example. When I say Rolls Royce, what do you think of?"

Thomas answered, "Expensive, high quality, luxury, exclusive—"

"Good. That's what they want you to think of. But they didn't get that brand recognition overnight. And they surely wouldn't have kept it if they delivered inferior products. A brand isn't just the logo, or emblem, though a company's identity is usually tied to those. What would come to mind if you saw a BMW logo?"

Thomas thought for a second. "That it was a high quality car."

The waitress stopped by to check on the table. "You all still okay?" Brad nodded and she sped away.

Robert pointed his butter knife and continued, "There are too many companies that have brand recognition issues. Either they don't know what they really stand for, which can confuse potential customers, or they create a brand but can't hold up the standard and the name gets tarnished or ruined."

Brad spoke up, giving Robert a chance to continue eating. "Customers view a brand as a direct promise." Take McDonald's, for example. "If you go to one of their restaurants anywhere in the country, you expect the same level of service, quality, and experience. When you see the golden arches, you have an expectation and they'd better meet it."

Robert added, "It doesn't matter where you are, what you order, whether or not it is in a bad location, or how busy they are—you want value and consistency."

"That's absolutely true," Thomas agreed.

The three men ate in silence for a moment. Thomas asked, "So, how did your paths cross?"

Robert took a big bite and washed it down with another sip of his coffee. He wiped his face with his napkin and began, "Well, I'll give you the short version, or we'll be eating lunch here as well." He leaned in to Thomas. "I'd been in real estate for about a year and hadn't been doing well at all, when I got a call to show a house our company had listed. It was in a pretty bad neighborhood and Brad was the man I met at the property. I had been struggling to get my name out and wasn't able to attract the kind of clients that would bring big commissions, so I was barely making ends meet. I drove up in my ten-year-old Toyota Corolla and Brad rolled up in a car that probably costs more than the house I was trying to sell." He took a sip of water, "I immediately pegged Brad for a slumlord who was trying to buy up a bunch of low-cost homes and use them as rental properties. Well, during the hour or so it took to show that house, I found out differently. My life changed dramatically that day." He smiled at Brad.

Robert looked a bit emotional but continued, "At that time in my life, I hadn't met Scott, nor had I gone through the Sensational Group training as you are doing now; I was just an inexperienced rookie who didn't know "Come here from sic 'em." Fortunately, I was the one who got the assignment to show that house. I opened the door to let Brad in, and when I turned around, he's climbing a half-dead tree in the front yard. After a few minutes, he got down and headed into the house without saying a word."

Brad laughed. "That definitely freaked you out."

Robert shook his head and continued, "True, but I calmed down. While showing the place, I began asking the standard questions, like "What do you plan to do with this place?" and "Will you need financing?" Brad never responded to any of them—it was like he was in a trance. So I pushed the throttle and asked him, "So what's your attraction to this house?" Brad jumped forward in his seat. "And that's when the floodgates opened."

Brad cast a deep look into Thomas's eyes and said calmly, "That's when I told him, 'This was the house my mother overdosed in.'" The three men sat silent for a moment. "I had to have that place. I wanted to right an old wrong, if you know what I mean." Thomas nodded.

Robert said, "After Brad shared his story with me, he says, 'Now, if you'll tell me your story, I'll pay asking price for this house.' What else was I going to do? I sang like a canary and told him everything he wanted to know."

"And a few things I didn't," Brad added.

The two men laughed and Robert went on, "So, I started just like you, just like most people who enter Brad's life do."

Thomas asked, "Are you guys partners in any businesses?"

"For sure," replied Robert. "Brad and I own a marketing and advertising company together."

"Unfortunately I have no stake in his real estate company," Brad said.

"So that's the secret to having ads everywhere," Thomas observed with a smile.

"Robert Nigh, the Real Estate Guy, has one of the best marketing and advertising campaigns around. And since we own all the available spaces, we get first shot at the ones with the highest visibility and traffic flow."

"That's pure genius," Thomas said quietly, with genuine admiration.

Robert looked at his watch. "I don't want to be rude, but I have a plane to catch—so enough about Brad and me. This is about you gaining a basic understanding of branding." The waitress cleared their dishes and he continued, "Sometimes brands are so strong in the marketplace that they become associated with an entire item category, no matter whose product it is." Thomas looked lost. Noticing this, Robert said, "Let me explain. Do you reach for a Q-tip when you need to clean your ears?"

Thomas answered, "Yes of course."

"Well, Q-tip is just one brand of cotton swab—but most people use that name to describe all swabs. How about Coke? I grew up in Atlanta, Georgia, home of Coca-Cola's world headquarters, and I happen to love that brand of cola drink."

Brad chuckled. "Me too."

"Now, when I was growing up, I drank RC Cola too," Robert continued. "But, throughout my life, I can't tell you how many times people would ask for a Coke, and when I handed them a Coca-Cola, they'd say, 'I meant a Pepsi.'"

Thomas nodded. "My grandma called every soda pop a Coke."

"I could go on and on. How about Kleenex or Clorox? Those are facial tissues and bleach, of which there are many brand names available in most stores."

"I've never said anything but Kleenex," Brad said.

"Now, when a company spends marketing money, they want the benefits, not the pitfalls. Think about it: Kleenex buys the ads, but other facial tissue companies may benefit. That's why companies spend money protecting their brands and products. They copyright and trademark their intellectual property because they want you to trust that if you buy their brand, you are getting an authentic product, not a knockoff or a replica." Robert took another sip of water, sat back, and continued, "So the moral of the story is to create a strong brand and protect it. Be proud and make sure people know what they can expect if they use your brand. Separate yourself and raise your standard higher than all of your competition. Constantly make them try to keep up with you. Then, as I said, protect and cherish it. Think about what ranchers do with their cattle: they brand them. It's so they can identify their own stock, and keep other people from stealing it.

Thomas asked, "What about the fact that you have your own brand, but you are also representing a brand like the Sensational Group? Does that ever pose a problem?"

Robert looked surprised. "Great question. Yes, it can be a huge problem. Co-branding can go very well or horribly wrong—I've seen both. You may have seen a Ford Explorer that's labeled an Eddie Bauer Limited Edition. In that instance, they are trying to create positive compounding with two products that have great names in their respective industries."

"Great brands have to be careful," Brad put in, "so that others don't water them down when joining forces."

"Great point," Robert continued. "Also, think about how many professional athletes have their own shoe or clothing line and then also get paid to represent a company like Rolex, or Buick. It's sad when you hear about an athlete doing something really stupid that not only embarrasses themselves and hurts their own brand, but also tarnishes the reputations of those other companies."

"Unfortunately, it happens all too often," Brad observed.

"I believe you must start with the idea that your brand is just as important as any company you may work for or represent.

Thomas spoke up, "My dad used to say, 'Protect the family name—it's the only one we have.'"

"Very well said," Brad said approvingly.

Robert went on, "You know, it's funny—no matter where you look, you can't find two humans who are exactly alike. At no time in the history of mankind have they been able to find two people with exactly the same fingerprint. Which confirms that you truly are unique. So, branding *you* should actually be just as important as branding any company, and it can be fairly easy."

Thomas joked, "Oh, I've already been branded by lots of people in my life."

Addressing Robert, Brad asked, "What time do you need to leave?"

Robert looked at his watch, "In just a few minutes. You don't have to be a famous athlete to focus on branding yourself. Look at me, for instance. I worked on my own brand even when I was employed by a realty company and doing projects for the Sensational Group. But I focused on keeping my standards high, keeping my name clean, and building my brand."

The waitress brought the check and Brad quickly snapped it up, handing it back with some cash.

Robert continued, "If you are a true sales professional and stick with it, it's possible you'll switch companies or products several times during your career. You may stay in the same field, but wouldn't it be nice if you gain a loyal customer base that ends up relying on you to solve their problems and follows you wherever you go?"

"Yes, that would be awesome," Thomas replied.

"Well, that will be determined by how your own brand is doing as well as who you work for. You'll get that commitment from people by making sure you have learned the skills to become one of the top professionals in your field. That's what this training is all about." Robert pulled out his smartphone and typed in his own name. He turned the phone to show it to Thomas. "You see, I'm Googleable. That means people can easily find me on the Internet. There are certainly other people in the world with the same name, but notice I come up first when I searched."

"And that's extremely important these days," Brad added. "I mean, when's the last time you opened a Yellow Pages?"

"Not since I was a kid," Thomas said.

"People will research you and your accomplishments before ever meeting with you. Prospective employers, customers, potential clients, investors, and possible employees will Google you."

The waitress brought Brad his change back, and practically in unison Thomas and Robert said, "Thanks for buying breakfast."

Thomas turned to Brad and asked, "But wouldn't it offend you if I were working on my own brand while training with your company?"

Brad took a moment. "*You* are Thomas every day, whether training with us, working for someone else, or doing whatever else comes along. If your individual brand is bad, it's going to negatively affect my company or someone else's at some point. So, I think you are always branding yourself, whether you realize it or not."

Robert interrupted, "Son, you are doing it right now. What I've been talking about is branding yourself on *purpose*!"

"Exactly," Brad interjected. "You are going to have a reputation regardless—I want you to develop a good one intentionally."

Robert began to gather his things. "Do you have your own website?"

Thomas shook his head. "No, sir."

"With the ease and cost of a website now, it only make sense to have your own web presence. Your page could contain your biography, a blog, or links to other great sites that would provide valuable content to those who find you. I realize there are other forms of social media, like Facebook or LinkedIn, but I'm talking about a true, stand-alone website. Imagine searching and finding www.ThomasFrickle.com. Having your own site will make finding you extremely easy." He stood. Brad and Thomas followed suit. "Hopefully it's not already taken, but if it is, use a middle initial, or hyphens."

As the three men headed out the door, Robert turned back to Thomas. "It's a small investment, and you can use one of the hundreds of free services or templates that are available. Put up success stories, achievements, your current job title, place of employment, and any areas of expertise. And now that you are working to be a high-quality sales professional, you won't believe how quickly people will take you seriously when you call for an appointment. It may take a little work, but go online and do some research. Many corporations have individual websites for upper management, board members, or the owners. Look at those and use what works for you." He offered his hand and shook the other men's hands in succession.

Brad smiled. "A true pleasure, as always. Thanks for working this into your schedule."

Thomas said, "Yes, thank you very much. I'm going to be a force to be reckoned with, thanks to you."

"You are more than welcome," Robert replied, "and I'll be searching for your website very shortly. You take care and we'll talk again soon." He turned and disappeared into the crowd of pedestrians. Thomas and Brad made their way to the car and drove to Thomas's house.

The car came to a stop, but Thomas didn't get out right away. Instead his face became serious.

Noticing this, Brad said, "Well, that's not the face of a sensational salesman."

Thomas tried to smile. "You taught me to be honest, right?"

"I hope so."

"I don't know how to say this without having it come out wrong."

Brad chuckled. "Man, just say it and we will sort through whatever comes out."

Thomas said slowly, "There's no way I could ever repay you for the education and training you are giving me, and I never want to seem ungrateful or disrespectful. So, that's why this is hard to say." He paused.

Brad urged him on. "Just spit it out."

Thomas drew in a deep breath and said, "I'm trying to go with the flow, but I'm starting to worry. I've got bills stacking up, and every day that goes by it's getting harder and harder to focus on the lessons. I'm running low on food, have no car, phone, or computer, and I never know what tomorrow is going to bring, except a new adventure and more knowledge."

Brad grinned and asked in a fatherly tone, "Who got you into this mess?"

Thomas lowered his head. "I know, I did. And I realize you are working to not only get me out of it, but to change my life for the better."

"Just look at how much you've accomplished without a car, phone, or computer. How much you've learned."

Thomas sat back. "That's very true. You know, last night Laura gave me a Rubik's cube and I had no idea how to solve it. So, I went to my neighbor's house, told him the truth, and explained what was going on. Would you believe it, he invited me in and let me use his computer for two hours to watch YouTube videos until I learned how. We both got the solution down pat. He told me he had wanted to learn how to solve those things since he was a kid."

Brad smiled. "Look, I know you are running on empty and it probably doesn't help when someone like Robert tells you to go and create a website. Have I let you down so far, or not upheld my end of the bargain?"

Thomas sighed. "No, sir, you've done everything you have said you would."

Brad patted him on the back. "Then just focus. You may only get one shot and you wouldn't want to add this opportunity to your list of regrets."

"No, that list is long enough already."

The two men climbed out of the car. Thomas was carrying his books as Brad walked him to the porch with an arm around his shoulder. "In life, the most committed usually wins. So, how committed are you?"

"Totally committed," Thomas said forcefully.

Brad stopped and looked him straight in the eyes. "You lost your job, your fiancée, car, phone, and most of your money and income.

And yet, I believe you have a solid future. I think you should be filled with hope. But all the effort you've put in will only pay off if you don't get sidetracked. You need to realize that this is only a short period in your life. If you lose this house, so what? And if you lose some weight because you don't have food, you'll become fitter."

Thomas grinned. "You always find the silver lining."

"Too many people give up on things when they are on the verge of success. That is where you stand today, on the verge. I sincerely hope you will finish the race."

"I will. I'm truly thankful for everything you are doing. I'm just in uncharted waters."

Brad laughed. "I've learned to accept that our entire lives are uncharted; that's what makes this so exciting and new." They shook hands. "The driver will be here at nine tomorrow morning," Brad said, then got into the car and drove away.

After a minute, Thomas went into the house, sat down in his reading chair, and opened the book Robert had given him. "Let's do this, Mr. Ginsberg," he said softly. He read until well after dark and finally fell fast asleep.

CHAPTER 15

Make the most of yourself, for that is all there is of you.
—Ralph Waldo Emerson

You Are the Business Card

Thomas awoke with a stiff neck, no feeling in one arm, and the book he was reading from Scott Ginsburg under his leg. He was disoriented; when he looked out the window it was very dark. He sat up so he could see the clock on the wall; it read 2:30. He slid out of the chair, headed to bed, and quickly fell back to sleep.

The next time he awoke, the air in the room was warm and still. He peered at the clock, which read 7:00, sat up, and noticed the sheets were soaked with sweat. He rose, walked over to the air conditioning thermostat, and found it in the off position. He shook his head. He was now trying to save money anywhere he could, and utilities were a good place to start.

After showering and getting ready, Thomas stood looking in the almost empty refrigerator. He pulled out a frozen waffle, placed it in the toaster, filled a glass with water, and wished Brad had shown up again to go to breakfast.

After eating, Thomas sat down and wrote in his journal. As he closed the book, he heard the limo pull into his driveway. He went to the door and looked out the peephole. Just as the driver was going to ring the bell, Thomas flung open the door and cried, "Good morning!"

The driver jumped back and grabbed his chest. "Good morning, Thomas. You almost gave me a heart attack." Thomas locked up and beat the man to the car, letting himself in the backseat before the driver climbed in and they drove off.

Thomas watched out the window as they drove through town and past the school where he had previously visited with Karl. The car stopped in front of a marble-covered building surrounded by palm trees. The sign read, SENSATIONAL SPA. The car door opened and Thomas stepped out. He was met by a beautiful Latina woman with a strong accent.

"Hello, Thomas, I'm Federica. I'm glad you are here today."

Thomas was a bit intimidated as he replied, "Nice to meet you, Federica. I like the name of this place."

She flashed a smile that looked as though she had twenty extra teeth, all perfectly straight and white. "Thank you. We should get started—this is going to take up most of the day." She led Thomas through the lobby to a small changing room. "There's a robe and slippers for you in there—go ahead and change into them, please. You can leave your things and lock the door behind you—don't forget the key."

It was Thomas's first time in a spa and he was uncomfortable. He changed, came out, and locked the door behind him.

Federica was waiting. "Now, other mentors may have told you their lesson would be the most important, but I think this one really is. And for some people it is difficult to accept. Do you want to reconsider? Now's your chance."

Thomas looked confident. "I'm okay with difficult, and I have a feeling whatever you share will help me." He clapped his hands. "Let's get this party started."

She added, "It's not hard to learn, just hard to hear sometimes." She led him down a hallway and into a large room where they were alone. "I'm glad you are eager and excited, because sometimes the truth hurts more than people are willing to admit. I'll be respectful, but this lesson usually comes with a big dose of criticism."

Thomas responded quickly, "Well, everything I do in my life now starts with the truth—if it hurts, so be it. I'm sure you don't find joy in hurting others." He winced. "And I say this with no disrespect, but I've learned recently that regardless of what you share with me, I can determine how I'll respond or what I'll feel."

She smiled. "Great! But don't be so confident or proud that you ignore professional advice."

Thomas laughed. "Never. I just wanted you to know that I am getting stronger every day and you don't have to worry about breaking me."

"What a fantastic response."

She walked him over to a huge mirror that was leaning against the wall and motioned to Thomas. "Go ahead and step in front." He looked into the mirror shyly. She said, "I'd like you to take a very close look at yourself—go ahead, from head to toe. What do you see?"

"I'm not sure what you mean. I see me in a robe and slippers, if that's what you're talking about." She didn't reply. "Well, I also see a guy who might need a makeover." Thomas laughed nervously.

Federica pause for a long moment and then said, "I'll tell you what I see." She walked right up to the mirror and pointed to Thomas. "I see a live business card that reads Thomas Frickle—and candidly, it's not of the highest quality." Thomas looked a little offended. "Remember, I'm not trying to pick on you. I'm going to be good for you, not necessarily good to you. Being critical is about critiquing."

He nodded. "Go on, I'll be fine."

She turned him around and said, "Forget about what you do for a living, or the title on your actual business card—that won't matter if you don't make some of what I feel are necessary changes. Before you have the chance to reach in your pocket and hand someone your paper card, they will have already judged you by what I call your *you* card. Unfortunately, it's how most of the world works."

"I agree one hundred percent. Although I'm working on not judging people by their looks, I'm sure lots of people do."

Federica went on, "Unless they are really organized or truly care, many people will use your business card to pick their teeth, as a bookmark, or to stick under the leg of a table or chair to help make it level. Many of them will probably lose it or throw it away. But no matter what happens to that card, I'm pretty positive they will never forget the impression you personally made on them—because in life, *you* are your business card."

Thomas nodded in agreement.

Federica sat Thomas down in a chair. "Have you ever put a Band-Aid on a cut or wound?"

Thomas looked puzzled. "Sure, lots of times."

"When it came time to remove it, did you pull it off slowly or rip it off quickly?"

Thomas thought for a second. "I guess I'm a *rip it off* kind of guy."

"Good, because though it's painful, you get it over quickly and move on to whatever is next, right?"

Thomas raised his eyebrows. "Yeah, I guess—but I'll be real honest, I'm not really up for a waxing."

She laughed. "Don't worry, I didn't plan one. However, I do want to go through the things that I feel you need to address, as quickly as possible, and hopefully any pain will go away just as fast."

"Okay, then, I'm ready when you are."

She began, "First, look at yourself again—and I realize you aren't in business attire right now, but pretend you are and ask yourself, Why would any customer or potential client buy from me versus my competition? Think about whether you look professional, trustworthy, or easily approachable. You don't need to share your list with me, just do it in your own head. Be honest and see how many unique answers you can come up with."

Thomas stared blankly for a few minutes and shook his head. "Pretty interesting. The more I think about it, I've never really looked at myself under a microscope before, even though I do it to other people all the time. I guess in the past if I was critical of myself, it produced self-doubt rather than a list of items to work on and improve. This would have been a deflating exercise a few weeks ago, but I understand the process of self-analysis more now and realize it's truly important for my improvement."

Federica replied, "Let's look at each individual aspect of what people will see when they meet you, and don't give me your answer when I ask. I want you to become totally aware of how you look. I also realize people have different styles and tastes, but some thing's are just not acceptable in any environment." She spun him around. "So first, check out your hair. Is it clean, any dandruff, is it smartly cut, or does it look like a mop? And when you talk about hair, it's not just from your point of view; look at the sides and back. Does your neck need to be trimmed? Believe it or not, if someone knows you take care of the things that aren't in your normal field of vision, they may believe you will give the same level of attention to their business or needs."

Thomas nodded. "Great point. If they see you're not detailed, then they might think you'll be the same way with them."

Federica smiled. "I have two children. When I send them to clean their rooms, one will do it perfectly, but the other will hide everything under the bed or in the closet. It may seem tidy at first glance, but when you begin to dig, it's a total wreck. That child simply tried to hide the problem. Don't ever hide anything.

"Let's keep ripping. So, again we don't have to discuss each item out loud, but ponder not only the hair on your head, but your facial and body hair as well. Guys tend to have issues with having too much as they get older. Many times, when it comes to eyebrows, ear, nose, back, or chest hair, it can get horribly out of control. It can be a huge distraction for other people." Thomas looked closely at the few hairs dangling out of his nostrils. She went on, "And under all that hair is skin. Is it dry, peeling, or even clean?" Shifting focus, she asked, "Do you know what women look at first on a man?"

Thomas chuckled. "Their wallets."

She sighed. "No, actually research shows it's hands." Thomas looked at his hands. "Are they clean, free from calluses? And how are your nails?" Thomas put his hands behind him.

Federica continued to uncover more of him. "Take a minute and smile big into the mirror."

Thomas smiled sheepishly, not proud of his teeth, "Some of us don't have a million-dollar smile, like you."

She closed her mouth for a moment and then said, "Perhaps not exactly like mine, but it can still be worth a million, if not more. You'll need to do the best with what you have. In fact, a genuine smile has more to do with your eyes than the showing of your teeth."

Thomas gave her a fake smile, with teeth only. "See, that's not a true smile. When a person is truly happy, they smile with their eyes, heart, and whole body in many cases. Your pretend smile will actually do more damage in a business setting. It will convey a message of insincerity—you will never build rapport with people who are always wondering why you aren't happy or trustworthy."

"I'm working on being truly happy. I'll give it another try when I have something to really smile about."

Federica tossed her hair in a flirtatious manner, turned coyly to look over her shoulder, ran her finger over his cheek, and in her sultry Latina accent whispered in his ear, "Ah, come on, Thomas, give me just one really good smile."

Thomas lit up like the Las Vegas Strip. She stepped back and said in her normal voice, "See, I knew you had it in you."

He shivered and laughed. "That's a pretty powerful weapon you have there. Your husband is a lucky man."

She nodded. "We are both lucky to have each other. I wasn't trying to be a tease, I just wanted you to get the idea."

Thomas smiled with his whole body. "Well, I did."

She cleared her throat. "Okay—let's get back to it. So, when it comes to those teeth, many people are self-conscious because their teeth are crooked, chipped, or stained. As I said before, do the best with what you have. Do you floss, use mouthwash, or carry breath mints? One of the toughest issues to figure out on your own is how your breath smells. I've met people whose breath hit me before I've had the chance to shake their hand, but they didn't realize it was a problem. Again, it's a distraction to others and, in my opinion, simply rude to put someone in an awkward situation. I mean, not many people want to tell you that your breath stinks. They usually just end the conversation quickly, and that's about the worst thing that can happen to a salesman."

"Right. If you have bad breath, whoever you are talking too won't hear a word you're saying and they can't wait to get away."

"Moving on, how about your clothes? How do they fit? Are they too tight or baggy? Are they clean and pressed? Do they have tears or buttons missing? Proper fit tells other people a lot about you. If they're too big, they wonder if you are trying to hide some extra weight, or has extra weight made them a little tighter? Do you care enough to have your clothes tailored when your weight changes, or can you afford it? Again, you are being judged. To be successful at what you do, you have to display specific signs. You have to give attention to detail and show that you care about your appearance. When you wear a belt, is it stretched, or does it have a permanent worn mark one or two holes away from where you have it buckled right now?"

Thomas said, "Belts are probably an issue for me. My weight fluctuates a bit, so I use different holes at different times of the year."

"My advice would be to have more than one belt, whether they are identical or just the same style and color. Belts aren't too expensive if you shop around and get them on sale. Have several—instead of changing holes when you gain five to ten pounds, just switch belts. People may not realize the extra weight, but they will realize that you've had to adjust your belt, or are using one that's too small."

"That's great advice. Most guys probably wouldn't think that way."

"When it comes to pants, I look at the bottoms of the legs to see if they have rips, tears, or strings hanging down. I see those flaws a lot. I realize people may not have the money to replace them, which is all the more reason to ensure that trouser legs are properly fitted, to prevent them from being stepped on." Thomas stuck his finger in the air to acknowledge this as "another item I'm guilty of."

Federica looked down at her feet. "And don't ask me why, but my biggest turn-off is dirty or worn-out shoes. Think about the pairs you own, are they unpolished or dirty, or are the soles worn unevenly? Although it's initially more expensive, buying high-quality shoes and taking good care of them will save you money in the long run, and make a better impression." They both sat silently for a moment.

Federica continued, "These are all things by which someone will be judging you within the first few seconds of a meeting. There is an old saying, "You only get one chance to make a first impression." Imagine handing someone your business card with the corner torn off, with coffee stains, maybe crumpled or with a crease in it. Your personal appearance is no different. Most decision makers will notice some or all of the things we've talked about almost immediately, and probably before you ever have a chance to say a word. So, their mind will be made up and you will begin the battle of trying to change it."

"I've faced that a lot in my life," Thomas replied. "And it's just about impossible to fix the situation when you start out on the wrong foot." Federica flashed her huge smile again.

"There's more," she continued. "How about your accessories? Do you carry a plastic ballpoint pen? Does it work, does it have advertising from another company on it, or even worse, has it been chewed on?" Thomas rolled his eyes with guilt. She leaned forward. "What about your satchel, briefcase, or computer bag? Is it worn out?"

Thomas was embarrassed. "Actually, it looks like it's been handed down from my grandfather."

There was a knock at the door and a young woman entered. She said, "Excuse me" and whispered something in Federica's ear, then left.

Thomas asked, "What was that about?"

Federica shrugged. "Nothing to worry about, let's continue."

She spoke slowly now, with a commanding voice. "Since we agree that you are the business card, then would you agree that how you speak is also a very important piece of the equation?" Thomas nodded in agreement. "Whether it's tone, pitch, volume, or the words you choose, how you talk and what you say will be key ingredients of your success."

"Wow—there's a lot to remember."

"The key is to make everything you do a habit, so you don't have to remember it. You need to get to the point where it just happens." He nodded. She moved her hand all over and around him, without touching him. "You see, it's everything that makes up who *you* are."

"Which will create my business card," he added.

She put her arm around him. "That's why all this is important. Think about it—are there reasons why certain people are picked to represent companies in commercials, ads, business meetings or transactions?"

"It's the whole package. How they look, what they say, how they carry themselves."

Federica nodded. "Exactly. Sponsorship dollars are huge, and they are awarded based on very specific criteria. Companies will also take away those contracts if their representative isn't doing what they are supposed to and showcasing the brand appropriately. Ask yourself whether, right this very minute, you would be proud to have yourself as a spokesperson for your own company. Whether you are the face, voice, model, boss, salesman—whatever your position, do you want the message and brand awareness to be resting on your shoulders?"

"I would probably hire someone else at this point," Thomas replied sadly.

She continued, "As you know, companies spend tons of money on branding. They work to put their best foot forward and promote their product in the shiniest possible light. Unfortunately, brands can also be tarnished in the blink of an eye. Please understand, no matter what company you work for, what product you are going to sell, even if you aren't going to meet people face to face—at some point customers will interact with someone from your company who represents the brand. They will hear his voice; determine how polite he is, whether his attitude is positive, and even how truthful he is. It's everything that makes up a brand for a company. And so, for you, it's everything about you that makes up your brand."

Federica pointed at Thomas in the mirror. "So, at all times, act as though you are your own business and your livelihood depends on you and you alone. Work toward improving your brand every day. Keep it healthy and polished. Imagine that *you* are your own business and it's going to be handed down to your children someday. What kind of brand will they inherit? Brad once asked me, 'If you were a company, would a man like Warren Buffet invest in you?'"

"He should now, because I'm on the rise," Thomas said.

Federica smiled. "And I would too. I think you have a very bright future." She looked at her watch and motioned for Thomas to follow her. "Let's go ahead and begin this transformation."

Federica took Thomas into the public area of the salon where there were several women getting their hair done. A young Asian woman greeted him. "Hello, Thomas, my name is Mylee and I'm going to give you a haircut. I hope you are ready. I've been looking forward to this all morning."

Federica chuckled. "Don't worry—she's fairly harmless."

Mylee grinned shyly and led Thomas to her chair. She took a moment to run her fingers through his hair. "You have very thick hair."

Thomas replied, "My dad used to say he didn't care if his hair turned gray, he just didn't want it to turn loose." They both laughed and she began putting a cape around him.

"Let's go get you washed." Thomas stood up and she guided him to a chair in front of a sink. He sat down and she began washing.

Thomas asked, "So, do you know what I am learning about today?"

Mylee answered, "Sure, that *you* are your business card."

Thomas pressed, "So, I guess that means you are helping to create mine." They giggled and chatted some more as she completed the task, towel dried his head, and took him back to her booth.

Mylee spoke as she began to cut, "Since this is about you being the business card, did you know that in many Asian cultures, the exchange of a business card is extremely important and sets the tone for the relationship? It's done with reverence; to anyone watching, it looks like a formal ritual or ceremony." Thomas shook his head. "They don't see the card as just a piece of paper with a name on it, but rather as an extension of that person and whom they represent."

"Looking back, I can't tell you how many people's business cards I threw away almost immediately. The way you put it, I guess I was really just discarding all those people and their companies."

Mylee added, "That's a good way to look at it."

Thomas sat up a little straighter and said, "You can bet from now on, I'll have reverence for theirs and my own."

"I once had a manager who said, 'Take each person's card and make notes on the back, something to remind you of the conversation and who they are.' It was a great idea and I still do it to this day."

As Mylee continued cutting, she went on, "Regardless of whether you put notes on them or not, you should keep each one. I not only saved the ones people gave me, but I also kept one from every position I've ever held during my work history. It's interesting to see my development, what companies I have worked for, and what the titles were along the way. It is a record of your professional progress." She spun Thomas around and handed him a mirror. "So, how do you like it?"

He looked at the front and back. "Very clean. It's a lot shorter than usual, but I love it."

166

She blew the hair off him with a blow dryer and began removing the cape. "So, the first stage is now complete. Are you ready to move on?"

Thomas smiled and glanced at his hair in the mirror, "I can't wait to see what's next."

Federica approached the two. "Looking good—you ready to keep it going?" Thomas smiled broadly as she escorted him to the manicure and pedicure area of the spa. As they walked she said, "Did you notice how enthusiastic and happy Mylee was as she cut your hair? That's one of the reasons she is usually booked out a month in advance. She not only gives people an awesome cut or style, but also makes them feel great while doing it. Excitement, enthusiasm, and passion are all traits and tools that will help you become successful in your professional career. So, on a scale from one to ten, how excited, passionate, or enthusiastic are you when talking to people?"

Thomas thought for a brief moment. "Probably not to the level I should be."

Federica continued, "Those characteristics are contagious. You can turn a bad situation around very quickly with just the right attitude. I know you have already learned about that—right?"

"For sure!"

They arrived at a large recliner with a jetted tub in front. A young woman helped him take his slippers off and motioned for him to step in the tub. He looked down toward his feet and became embarrassed.

Federica chuckled. "Thomas, this is Sarah. She's going to make your hands and feet look as good as your new haircut." Sarah looked up and nodded in agreement.

Thomas shrugged. "Well, then, she has her work cut out for her."

"You'll continue to get the royal treatment. She has lots more to teach you."

Thomas looked around the room. "I'll have to admit, this is an incredible team of people you have here."

"Bear in mind, we only provide additional education to those who are in the program. Both Mylee and Sarah have worked for other companies under the Sensational umbrella, but they love being here and serving clients in this way."

"It makes total sense to address these topics here in this environment," Thomas observed.

Federica grinned. "Very true. Now sit back and let both the pampering and lessons continue."

Sarah began scrubbing Thomas's feet. He watched her work diligently. "You seem to really enjoy it here," he said.

Sarah glanced up. "Certainly. We all love what we do. I'm sure Mylee was very happy too, right?"

"She was very enthusiastic."

Sarah paused, then said, "Now it's my turn to ask a question. How do you come across to other people when you are doing your job? Are you happy and easy to be around, or are you a Debbie downer?"

Thomas thought for a second. "Well, I'd like to think I'm not a Debbie downer, as you say, but I'm probably not as upbeat as everyone around here."

Sarah switched to Thomas's other foot. "So, what about when you aren't physically in front of someone as we are now?" Thomas looked puzzled. "There are lots of other ways people communicate. Like when you send email, or use a phone. Have you thought about how you come across to people when you write something?" Thomas shook his head no and she went on, "And here's something not many people give much attention to: the greeting on their voice mail. Think about all the messages you have left on other people's phones. Were you upbeat, enthusiastic—was there passion in your voice?" Thomas pondered this question as she continued, "Now I don't mean you have to go overboard, but do they understand by your words, tone, and volume that you love what you do? Are you someone people really look forward to talking to?"

Thomas replied, "Now you have me thinking. I would hope so, but I'm not so sure."

Sarah began working on Thomas's hands. She noticed a small blister and some calluses. "What are these from?"

Thomas examined his hands curiously. "I'm not sure. I could have got them from all the writing I've been doing and the notes I've been taking lately, or possibly when I helped clean up a park recently."

"We'll take care of it, and since you mentioned writing, how is your penmanship?"

Thomas looked embarrassed. "It horrible."

"Unfortunately nice, legible handwriting is almost a forgotten art form and an area that people overlook fairly often. If you have to write orders, or notes to other people, it's imperative that your handwriting be legible. As a salesman, it should be your standard practice to write thank-you or follow-up cards to each person you deal with. It's a habit that will set you apart. Sending something handwritten after a meeting really shows you care. But you have to be careful, many people will look at something you wrote, and if it's sloppy, they'll assume you will handle all your work that way."

"I could easily see that happening," Thomas replied.

The two were startled when a young woman sneezed and a chorus of "bless you's rang out. Sarah asked, "That reminds me, do you carry a hanky, or Kleenex?"

"Neither one consistently."

She pursed her lips. "I guess carrying a hanky might not be as acceptable as it once was. Mainly because of the way the media and public focus on germs. No one wants to be offered a cotton rag full of your—well, you know what I mean." They both giggled. "But you could always carry a small package of facial tissue." She looked around, "I'd even be willing to bet most of the women in here have one with them now."

Thomas nodded. "That's probably true, knowing all the stuff my mom carried in her purse." He sighed deeply. "Federica was right—this lesson has the most details to learn and think about."

"If you can remember and apply all of them, you'll stand out as a sensational salesman, as well as a true gentleman." Thomas sat up straight and breathed deeply.

Sarah continued buffing his nails and offering more of her wisdom. "A good friend of mine often says, 'Chivalry isn't dead, it just sleeps most of the time.' It's up to guys like you to wake it up. Many times people think you only need to act courteously, kindly, or politely in the presence of a lady. I believe you will truly stand out—you know, really separate yourself from the crowd—if you behave the same toward both men and women."

Thomas winced as Sarah clipped his cuticles. "Sorry! This is the first manicure I've ever had."

Sarah laughed, "They'll get easier if we stay on top of it. In fact, you may even like it someday." She rubbed some ointment on the tender area and wiped off the excess with a towel. At that moment Federica returned.

Sarah stood. "Well, he's moving in the right direction, that's for sure." She helped Thomas up.

Federica motioned ahead of her. "And the journey continues. Let's head to my office."

Thomas glanced back toward Sarah. "Thank you very much. I'll come see you again for sure." He turned and followed the clickety-clack of Federica's heels all the way to her office.

Entering, he took a seat and asked, "How many other men have you turned into gentlemen?"

Federica laughed, "A few hundred. I like to think of myself as a sculptor. There's a gentlemen within every man; the excess just needs to be chiseled away to reveal the good stuff."

Federica opened a book on her desk, took a pen, wrote something, and presented it to Thomas. "This should help you remember some of the things we've talked about today, and help you become a sensational salesman." Thomas ran his finger across the title, "The Perfect Gentleman." He stammered, "I—I really appreciate this. I'll continue striving to be the best I can be."

She nodded. "There's a lot of good information in that book. My husband and son have both read it several times and they regularly practice just about everything in there." She giggled. "They are still working on the perfect part." Thomas chuckled as well. Federica went on, "Probably the most important thing I got out of reading the book is that being a gentleman isn't just about how you treat women, it's about how you treat everyone, including yourself."

Federica glanced at her watch. "Well, there's one more surprise for today." Thomas looked eager to find out what it was as the two left the room yet again. Federica led him down a different hallway and into a room with a massage table in the middle. She motioned to him to enter. "This should make you feel awesome. Although we want you to relax, Tonya will share some of her thoughts with you. When you are done, she'll show you to the changing room and then we'll meet to say goodbye."

Thomas nodded. "See you in a while."

As Federica left the room, Tonya entered and pointed to the table. "I'm going to step back outside for a minute and let you get ready. You can hang your undergarments and robe on the door, climb up, and lie on your stomach, with your face in the donut hole."

Thomas looked uncomfortable. "So, totally naked, then?"

Tonya grinned, "Yeah, but you'll be under the covers, and I've done this more times than I can count. It'll be okay."

He did as she instructed, and before he knew it she was back and turning on some soothing music. She began to rub his back with some warm oil. "I usually don't talk during a massage," she said, "but, as you know, we are also here to instruct you. I hope it won't keep you from relaxing."

Thomas was beginning to loosen up, and though it was uncomfortable to speak through the opening, he said, "Since it's my first time, I wouldn't know what's normal or not. So, just do whatever you usually do and I'll cooperate."

She pulled the covers down a bit to work on his lower back. "There's a good chance you won't remember everything you've heard here today, but I see Federica gave you the book, so you can go over it all again whenever you want." Thomas tried to nod. "There are aspects of being a gentleman that sometimes get overlooked," Tonya continued. For instance, hat etiquette. Some people think it's old fashioned, but removing your hat when you meet someone, step indoors, or sit down to eat can really set you apart." Thomas mumbled in agreement as she moved on to his arms.

The song in the background changed as she continued working on him. "So many courtesies that people think are only supposed to be done by a man for a woman, could easily be done for anyone. Like opening a door or offering to help someone take off or put on a coat. The men who are kind and thoughtful to everyone equally are the ones I believe are the true gentlemen. If a man acts in a distinctive manner that's different from the crowd, people will gravitate toward him. So, if you are working to be a sensational salesman, and are your own business card, then why not be the best they have ever come across?" Thomas mustered up a half-hearted response as drool began to drip from the corner of his mouth and onto the floor. "Let's get you turned over," she said.

Thomas rolled over and kept his eyes closed. She began massaging his chest. "You'll find just about anything you need in that book. There are chapters full of ideas and pointers to help you look great and save money at the same time. I've actually used it to help decide what gifts to buy people. In fact, I've given the book to several people, and I can tell that it's had a positive effect on them."

Thomas opened one eye. "What kinds of gifts?"

"Shoe shine kits, for instance, and collar stays for dress shirts. Oh, speaking of dress shirts, you should always wear an undershirt to keep from staining the armpits. And here's a little known fact: if you'll have the cleaners use light starch, shirts last twice as long. Too much and it will quickly eat up the buttons." She moved around to work on his head and face. I'm not sure how many people really notice the details, but I do."

Thomas sighed deeply. "Looking back, I'm sure most of the people I dealt with in my last job noticed. Now that I'm learning what it means to be a professional, it's easy to see my shortcomings. I'm sure I lost or never got business because of my business card at that time. Those people probably took one look at me and thought, *If that's how he takes care of himself, then he'll probably make a mess of anything we give him to do.*" She rubbed his ears and Thomas smiled contentedly.

Tonya whispered, "It's worth repeating the old phrase, 'Customers don't care how much you know until they know how much you care.' There's a lot of truth in that. Proper appearance will get the ball rolling in the right direction, but then you have to follow that with everything else people notice. For instance, how punctual are you normally?"

"Let's just say I have lots of room for improvement."

"When I was out calling on customers, I'd get to my appointments early every time. You can find somewhere close by, eat a bite, do some work, or just wait for the appointment time to arrive. Sure, I had traffic issues, and flat tires, but those things never ruined my schedule. In fact, when I would tell a customer about my difficulties and they realized that I had a horrible time getting there but still made my appointment—because I planned and prepared for the worst—they respected me and knew I'd be the same way with their business."

Tonya began massaging his face. "There are some things that aren't in that book that definitely should be; perhaps there will be another edition. For instance, there is no mention of phone etiquette. Whether it is how you speak, the messages you leave for others, or the outgoing message on your answering machine, it's all part of your business card."

"Sarah mentioned that earlier. I know my messages are boring."

"They shouldn't be. They need to distinguish you from the millions of other salesman, so when people hear it, they can't wait to talk to you." She began wiping off the excess oil from

Thomas's face. "And there is no mention of fitness or diet." She noticed Thomas was becoming uncomfortable. "You know none of us are as fit as we want, but eating right, drinking enough water, sleeping well, working out—all of those things will help us perform better.

She went on, "I am probably one of the most overprepared people you will ever meet. I do things like regularly update my GPS. I also carry a ton of stuff in my shoulder bag, like extra change, office supplies, medicines, a toothbrush—you name it and I probably have it. And trust me, it regularly comes in handy. Usually when someone else needs something."

Thomas laughed. "You sound like the kind of person everyone needs around them."

"That's exactly what I am hoping for," Tonya replied.

She finished wiping off Thomas's face and her hands. "I love it when customers say things like 'You are really different' because it opens the door for me to ask them questions."

Thomas was curious. "Like what?"

She obliged. "Like, Is it a good or bad thing that I'm different? Or, In what way am I different?" Those questions might give you valuable feedback that you may not get otherwise. If they say, I never had someone treat me so well or be so polite, then you know you are definitely on to something good."

Thomas confessed sheepishly, "I've probably been different for all the wrong reasons, but I'm turning that around now thanks to people like you."

Tonya smiled. "Well, that's it for me. I'll leave and allow you to get back into your robe. Then you can just head back to your changing room to get dressed. Do you remember where it is?"

Thomas replied, "Yes, just down the hall."

"I'll let Federica know you are getting dressed, and don't forget your book."

Thomas smiled warmly. "Thank you very much for the massage and the lesson. They were both much needed."

As Thomas was getting dressed in the changing room, he heard a very familiar voice speaking in the hallway outside his door. He stood frozen as he heard Sandy say, "I definitely need this massage. The last couple of weeks have been the worst of my life."

"I'm sorry to hear that," Tonya replied. "I'll do my best to help you relax."

Thomas stood there in his changing room until they walked off. Slowly opening the door, he peeked out to find Federica standing alone in the hallway.

"Are you all dressed?" she said, noticing him.

He stepped out carefully and answered quietly, "Yes, ready to go. Is there anything else we need to cover?"

She pointed to the book. "I think whatever we didn't cover you'll find in there."

As they walked to the front and passed the closed door to the room where Sandy was getting a massage, Thomas had an overwhelming sense of sadness. They reached the front and he could see the car waiting outside for him. He turned and, in a low voice, thanked Federica and the other women who were in the reception area before heading out the door and into the limo.

Thomas was silent during the entire drive. All he could think about was what Sandy had said. He wanted to do or say something, but he just didn't know yet how to handle the situation. Hearing her voice and almost bumping into her helped him determine to start focusing on how to handle it, because he wanted to make things right with her. They pulled into the driveway and Thomas opened the door before the car came to a stop.

The driver got out of the car and followed Thomas toward the house. "Mr. Thomas, I'll be dropping a tuxedo by in the morning."

Thomas looked surprised. "So, back in the old penguin suit again?"

"Yes, sir, and I will return later in the afternoon to pick you up for a special event."

Thomas was interested. "Special event?"

The driver grinned. "Well, it is your final day in the program."

"Thank you for making two trips on a Sunday," Thomas called after him. I really appreciate everything you are doing for me."

The driver waved. "You are welcome." He climbed into the car, and slowly slipped out of the neighborhood. Thomas waited until he had left before shutting the front door and exploding into a crazy happy dance.

CHAPTER 16

The best way to find yourself is to lose yourself in the service of others.

—Mahatma Gandhi

Leaving a Legacy of Giving and Serving Others

The clock read 4:45, and Thomas lay in bed wide awake. He was so excited that this was to be the last day of his training. He had his heart set now on a position with the company; didn't care where it was, as long as he had a place. He felt so at home, and knew he would do a great job now that he had his head on straight. Thomas began to slow down and think of all the lessons he had been taught. He quickly focused, cleared his mind, and lay there in bed counting his blessings for hours until he heard the car drive up. He met the driver and thanked him for bringing the tuxedo.

Thomas spent the day reflecting on everything that had happened over the last couple of weeks. He sat writing and rewriting letters to Sandy, his parents, and Brad. He planned to give Brad his letter at some point during the evening. Thomas took a break in the afternoon and went for a walk around the neighborhood. Looking at each house, he thought about holding a party in the future to get to know all his neighbors. When he got back home, he went through the entire checklist on good grooming as he prepared for the evening. It helped that he had just been to the spa. He dressed and stood so he wouldn't wrinkle his clothes until the driver finally arrived. Thomas climbed into the backseat of the limo and they headed off.

The driver seemed to be proceeding very slowly, but Thomas didn't want to ask why, just in case it was some kind of a test. So he sat quietly until the car finally pulled to a stop in front of the civic center. He could read the sign outside: THE SENSATIONAL GROUP'S SEVENTH ANNUAL AWARDS GALA. By now it was dark and there were klieg lights dancing around the sky as though a Hollywood red carpet event were taking place. Oddly enough, there were no other people around the entrance. The door to the car swung open, and as Thomas exited, a lovely woman stepped out of the center to greet him. She offered her arm and escorted him into the building. They quickly entered an enormous banquet room that was jam-packed with people seated at an ocean of tables.

Thomas was the last guest to enter the room, which was filled to capacity. As he got closer to the front, he noticed all his mentors were sitting together at a couple of tables. The attendant led Thomas to a table in the center of the room, right in front of the stage. Brad, Brad's wife, Victor, and several other people Thomas didn't recognize were already seated. Just as he began to say hello to everyone, a gentlemen adorned with a colorful bow tie and socks stood up from the table and said, "Well, I guess it's show time. Wish me luck." The man made his way to the stage and took the microphone in his hand.

Thomas looked at everyone at the table and whispered, "Good evening—sorry I'm late."

Brad smiled. "Your timing is perfect. We'll do introductions in a little while."

The man on the stage began, "Good evening, ladies and gentlemen. My name is Anthony Belser. Most people know me by my stage name, Tone-X, or by my other name, The Sock King."

He raised his pant leg to reveal his colorful socks and the crowd cheered. "Tonight it is my distinct honor to have been chosen as MC for the Sensational Group's Seventh Annual Gala Awards Fundraiser, and I'm going to do my best to provide you with some laughs throughout the evening. I'm also positive you are going to be enlightened and entertained by the other guests who will grace this stage tonight. Now, as most of you probably know, tonight's event is the creation of one very humble and giving man. I'll give him a break and just ask that he stand where he's at, so we can acknowledge him. He will be coming up later tonight to present this year's Sensational Award. Please help me give a warm round of applause for the man who makes this happen each year, Mr. Brad Williams." Brad reluctantly stood and waved to the crowd with a look of humility and embarrassment, then quickly sat back down.

Once the cheers and applause stopped, Tone-X continued, "As you know, each year the Sensational Group selects a different nonprofit organization to support. This year, the money raised from tonight's gala event will be going to the SKIP1 organization. If you aren't familiar with them, don't worry—you will be soon enough. But before we get to that, I'd like to bring to the stage an incredibly talented young entertainer whose voice will surely leave you spellbound. You may remember her from the first season of *X-Factor*. Please help me welcome to the stage Ms. Drew Ryniewicz."

Thomas sat in awe as a young woman who was seated at his table rose and made her way to the stage. She sang a couple of her newly released songs and the crowd went wild. The applause continued until she returned to her seat near Thomas. Tone-X addressed the crowd again, telling jokes for a couple of minutes before moving on. The waiters were now bringing around the appetizer; yet, there wasn't the usual clatter of glasses and silverware typical of events like these.

Tone-X continued, "Our next guest is an incredible woman with a very powerful message, the founder of the Women's Prosperity Network and the author of several books, including *The One*

Philosophy. Please help me welcome Ms. Nancy Matthews." Again Thomas was surprised when a rather tall woman who had been sitting at his table stood and confidently strode up the stairs to the middle of the stage.

With a hint of a Brooklyn accent, she addressed the audience. "Thank you for the warm reception. It's an honor to be here tonight surrounded by so many incredible people." Nancy went on to explain that the ONE philosophy was about showing up and being the one for other people every day of your life. She said, "You need to open yourself up to the world of possibilities by focusing on being empathetic and supporting of others."

Thomas looked around the room at the other guests and at the people at his table. He couldn't believe he was here in this setting. It was like a dream come true. For a moment, he felt a sense of guilt, thinking he didn't deserve this because of the way he had behaved in the past—and especially because of how things had gone with Sandy.

Nancy continued by sharing a very touching story of a waitress who was having a bad day until some customers decided to take an interest in her. They worked hard to bring a smile to her face; when they were leaving, they gave her a substantial tip and lots of hugs. They made sure she knew that what she did mattered and that they cared about her well-being. Returning to the restaurant two weeks later, they were served by the same waitress. She told them that she had been considering suicide the night they treated her so well, and it was because of their compassion that she found a reason to live. The audience was visibly moved, and Nancy challenged everyone to be the ONE for someone, anyone, every day. Tone-X returned to the stage and the audience gave her a long and booming round of applause as she departed.

The waiters were now clearing the appetizer plates and began serving the salads. Tone-X continued telling jokes. As Nancy sat back down at the table, she reached over and grabbed Thomas's hand in a reassuring way. He smiled from ear to ear. Tone-X continued, "Our next guest doubles as a huge teddy bear when not speaking to audiences." The crowd laughed. "But on the real, he is one of the most giving people you will ever meet and he is here to teach us all how to be Go-Givers. Please welcome Mr. Bob Burg."

A very tall man with an infectious smile stood up from Thomas's table and made his way to the stage. Thomas was astonished at the fact that every speaker so far was sitting at his table. He was enjoying every presentation, but he also couldn't wait for them to be over, so he could spend some time talking to each of them.

Mr. Burg explained that he had written a book titled "The Go-Giver" with John David Mann. He shared the five laws from the book: 1. Your true worth is determined by how much more you give in value than you receive in payment. 2. Your income will be determined by how many people you serve and how well you serve them. 3. Your influence is determined by how abundantly you place other people's interests first. 4. The most valuable gift you have to offer is yourself. And finally, 5. The key to effective giving is to stay open to receiving. Each lesson was a revelation to Thomas and he hung on Bob's words. When he was finished, the crowd erupted again. Tone-X returned to the stage and Bob took his seat back at Thomas's table.

The waiters began clearing the appetizer plates as Tone-X introduced yet another speaker. "Now, the lady I'm about to bring to the stage is one of the most high-energy, make-things-happen kind of people I have ever met, and if her story doesn't hit you right between the eyes, I'm going to have my bodyguards come and do it. Please welcome to the stage the founder of the Skip1 organization, Mrs. Shelene Bryan.

An energetic blond woman stood up from Thomas's table and made her way to the stage. As she arrived, a legion of waiters and waitresses began lining up around the edge of the room with covered plates in each hand, holding the surprise entrée everyone was about to receive.

Shelene began, "Hasn't this evening been incredible? On behalf of Skip1.org, I am deeply grateful to all of you for attending. Your contributions tonight will help feed children in Uganda, run a hospital in Peru, and educate kids in Costa Rica. Now, many times people ask why we aren't helping here in our own country—and I'm proud to say that we do. In fact, we have just partnered on a men's rehabilitation center in San Francisco to match the women's shelter we opened in 2008." The audience gave her a huge round of applause.

"And just so you know, every dollar donated or raised goes directly to the people who need it most. The primary goal of Skip1 is to create awareness and teach people to be grateful for what they have, and to share with others to ease their suffering or give them a leg up in life." The army of waiters began moving into position around each table. "So tonight," Shelene continued, "Since we all have already enjoyed an appetizer and a delicious salad—" She paused as the waiters put down the plates and removed the covers to reveal pictures of people instead of food. "—I'm asking each of you to skip this one entrée to help someone in need." The audience erupted in applause and gave Shelene a standing ovation.

When she finished with her presentation, the crowd cheered. Many people came forward and begin tossing donations onstage. Tone-X came up beside her once again and thanked everyone as Shelene returned to her table. As the crowd settled down, Tone-X continued, "Ya'll are going to make me strip down to my G-string and try to earn some money up in here. I hope someone knows how to make it rain for me." Everyone laughed, and he turned serious. "Now, I think we would all agree this has been a magical night so far. And, if you all are ready, I'd like to bring Mr. Brad Williams to the stage, so we can find out who will be the recipient of this year's Sensational Award."

Brad made his way up the steps and Tone-X handed him the microphone. Quietly, two men came from backstage with a table and another followed carrying a trophy.

Brad began, "Several years ago I met a man who was truly sensational. Unfortunately, he passed away before I had the opportunity to tell him how I felt or give him the recognition he so richly deserved. That incident led me to create the award I am presenting here tonight. I am surrounded by many awesome people who all deserve awards." He motioned to the trophy. "But this one is presented to someone who has shown himself to be a true inspiration and hero in his community." He pulled out some notecards, paused, and then chuckled as he threw them onto the floor behind him.

"I'm not sure why I made notes. I could talk for hours about this year's recipient." Brad looked directly at a man sitting across from Thomas for a very long time and then became visibly emotional. He gathered himself and continued, "I have known this year's award winner for many years. From the moment we met, I knew there was something very special about him. For one, he has always taken the high road with people, no matter what the circumstances. If you were to meet him today, you might think he has always had it easy in life because of his incredible attitude, but he hasn't. This is a man who lost everything, and decided with his supportive wife to face his fears head-on. When his homebuilding business went under, he could have filed for bankruptcy, but instead he vowed to pay back every dollar to every person he owed."

Brad pulled out a handkerchief and wiped his face. "This is a man who tithed ten percent, even when he needed that money for other things. He sold off a car and donated the money to charity, started a nonprofit to help needy children, and is constantly there to provide advice or an encouraging word to those around him. Because of his willingness to *give and serve* others, he is *leaving a sensational legacy.*" Brad took another long look at the man seated across from Thomas. "As I said, I could go on and on about this guy, but I'd end up a total wreck. So, without any further delay, it is my distinct honor to present this year's Sensational Award to Mr. Kenneth Ray Belcher."

The man across from Thomas stood and began making his way to the stage. Everyone including the wait staff gave him a standing ovation. Brad met him with a big hug, and then handed him the trophy and microphone. The room grew perfectly silent as Mr. Belcher addressed the crowd for a few minutes. He ended by thanking everyone profusely before humbly leaving the stage to another standing ovation.

Tone-X softly spoke into the microphone, "Well, ladies and gentlemen, I hope you will leave here as inspired as I am. On behalf of Brad Williams, the Sensational Group, and Skip1.org, we thank you for your attendance, your support, and we hope you will join us here again next year. Have a safe journey wherever you are headed, and Peace and Blessing to you all."

Thomas noticed everyone at his table remained as Tone-X returned. As people filed out of the building, they stopped to thank the speakers and congratulate Mr. Belcher. Slowly the room began to empty and Brad addressed the table. "Well, everyone, I want to thank you for your participation—it was definitely a night to remember. I'd also now like to introduce you to the newest member of the Sensational Group, Thomas Frickle." Brad motioned toward Thomas and the people at the table clapped and congratulated him.

Brad continued, "His first official day is tomorrow, so he may need to get out of here soon and get some rest." Everyone laughed and then became quiet. Brad turned to look Thomas in the eyes. "But first I think there is some unfinished business you need to take care of." Brad pointed to a table across the room where a woman who looked like Sandy was sitting all alone.

Thomas could hardly catch his breath and asked, "Is that?—"

Brad nodded. "It is. Why don't you go speak to her? She's been here the whole evening."

Thomas looked back and forth between Sandy and Brad. "I don't know how—but *thank you.*" Addressing everyone at his table, he said, "I apologize for not being able to spend more time with you tonight. I would really love to get to know you better. But as you can imagine, there is something I must attend to, and it won't wait any longer." They all nodded with understanding as Thomas excused himself and made his way over to Sandy.

She turned to face him just as he arrived. Thomas grinned. "Good evening, my name is Thomas Frickle. What's yours?"

Sandy gave a hint of a smile and said, "Sandy Hill."

"Are you getting ready to leave, or may I sit down?"

"I have some time, if you'd like to sit."

Thomas sat down, then turned his chair to face her. He looked deep into her eyes. "This might sound a little crazy, but I was wondering if I could tell you my story."

She smiled widely. "I think I'd like that."

CPSIA information can be obtained at www.ICGtesting.com
Printed in the USA
LVOW11s0758190315

431096LV00001B/1/P